Moroccan

Moroccan

Rachael Lane

Contents

Introduction

In Morocco, the pleasure of eating food is equal to the pleasure of sharing it. Moroccan hospitality is evident from the moment you set foot inside a family home. After a warm greeting, you may even receive a dousing of perfume or scented water. Meanwhile, family members will be busy finishing their final preparations for the feast to come.

In this book there are more than 120 inspiring recipes to help you create your own Moroccan feasts. You can try simple grilled kebabs or the lavish, celebratory chicken bastilla. Make your own succulent tagines and piles of fluffy couscous covered with mouth-watering stews, as well as cleansing soups and salads, seafood and meat dishes, and tempting selections of Moroccan sweets. Extras include classic Moroccan flavorings, preserved lemons and harissa paste, and to conclude your feast, the traditional method for preparing mint tea.

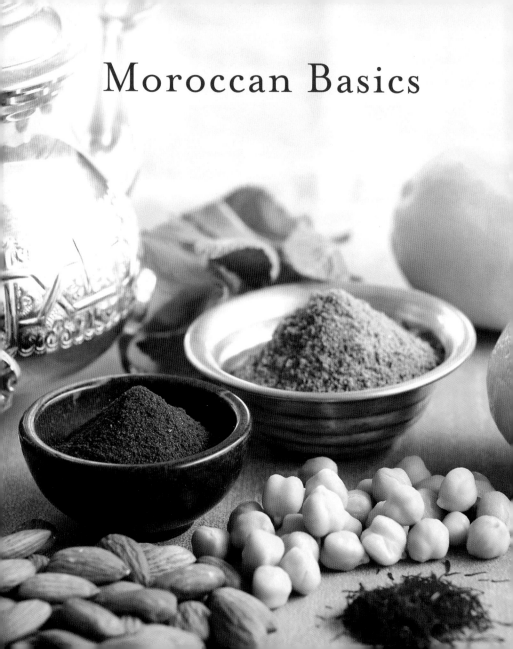

Moroccan Basics

Morocco borders the Atlantic Ocean and the Mediterranean Sea. In the coastal regions fish and seafood can be found in abundance. The more fertile land is in the north, where the majority of citrus and other fruits, nuts and olives are grown. The south is more arid as a result of the Sahara desert with few crops being grown there.

Moroccan cuisine has been influenced over the centuries by the indigenous, mainly Muslim, Berber population. Spanish, Portuguese, French, Moorish, Middle Eastern, Mediterranean and African influences are also present and have helped shape the cuisine.

Main Ingredients

The marketplace is at the heart of Moroccan cuisine. These open-air stalls are alive with the fragrance of fresh herbs and pungent spices, the clatter of tea glasses on silver trays and eye-catching displays of intricately painted tagines and serving dishes, not to mention piles of gleaming fresh produce. The food section has everything a Moroccan kitchen needs, from fresh, dried and preserved produce to meat, poultry and fish. Other treats include large bullet-shaped cones of compacted sugar sold in bulk for sweetening mint tea, Chinese green tea, bottles of scented rose- and orange-blossom waters and tubs of wild honey.

As the Moroccan market shows, the key to Moroccan cooking is 'fresh is best'. The ingredients used in the recipes that follow are available from fresh food and specialty markets. Alternative ingredients are suggested for the more unusual items.

VEGETABLES AND FRUIT

A bountiful array of fresh and seasonal produce is used in Moroccan cooking. The most widely used vegetables and fruits are red onions, tomatoes, root vegetables (such as potatoes, sweet potatoes, turnips and carrots), artichokes, okra, various types of lettuce, citrus fruits, red and green grapes, and stone fruits such as peaches, plums and nectarines.

HERBS

Fresh herbs are used in abundance, particularly flat-leaf parsley and cilantro, and mint for making tea – if fresh mint is not available, sometimes dried mint is used.

MEAT, POULTRY AND SEAFOOD

Meat, poultry and seafood are used in tagine and couscous dishes, and special occasions may include a course of stuffed or slow-roasted meat, poultry or fish. Meat is often coarsely ground to make kefta for kebabs, or to fill briouats (fried pastries) or fried breads. Most commonly eaten are chicken, lamb and mutton, goat, and beef. In the south it is common for camel to be eaten as well. Since Morocco is a Muslim country, pork is not seen on the menu, and all meat is halal in accordance with Islamic law.

DRY GOODS

Essential dry goods in Moroccan cooking include: semolina grains for making couscous, pastries and breads; chickpeas; lentils; dried beans, especially broad beans and green beans; rice;

dried fruits such as dates, figs, raisins, apricots and prunes; and nuts and seeds such as almonds, sesame seeds, walnuts and peanuts.

SPICES AND FLAVORINGS

Moroccan cooking is characterised by its fresh, zesty and spicy flavors. Essential to this are green, black and purple olives; preserved lemons; fiery red harissa paste; chermoula paste; and fruity olive oils.

The spicing of Moroccan cuisine is always subtle, not over-powering – spices are even used in sweet dishes. The main spices used are cumin, ginger, paprika, turmeric, black pepper, saffron, chili powder, star anise, cinnamon and nutmeg.

There are four spice mixes that are commonly used as bases for tagine sauces. These are also used to flavor roast meats or couscous. They are:

· k'dra – a pale-yellow sauce made from butter, onion, saffron, white pepper and ground ginger

- m'charmel – a mixture of other sauces, generally red in color, which often contains saffron, black pepper, red chili powder, ground ginger and cumin
- m'hammer – a red sauce based on butter, paprika and cumin
- m'qualli – a yellow sauce containing ground ginger, saffron and oil

Cooking & Equipment

When buying a tagine dish, make sure you choose the appropriate one for your requirements. Some tagines, particularly the highly ornate ones, are designed for presentation only. Other tagines are made to withstand the heat of hot coals, the stove top and the oven.

If you don't have a tagine for cooking, it is still possible to make a tagine. Simply use a flameproof or ovenproof dish. Follow the recipe's instructions and cook on the stove top or in the oven at a low–medium temperature for approximately the same amount of time.

In Morocco, a couscoussier (a large pot consisting of two sections) is traditionally used for cooking couscous. A steamer saucepan can be used instead with satisfactory results. Line the perforated steamer base with cheese cloth to prevent the small couscous grains from falling into the broth below. Or fit a colander over a pot and seal the outer edges with aluminum foil to make sure the steam only escapes upwards to cook the couscous.

There is quite a knack to preparing couscous in the traditional Moroccan way. Grains are gently steamed, separated and dried, and the process is repeated, before the couscous is served with its accompanying broth or stew. Follow the instructions for traditional couscous on page 54 or, if time is short, use instant couscous – directions are on the package.

Starters

Ever-popular kebabs and keftas can be seen cooking over hot coals at open-air restaurants and markets throughout Morocco. They are sold as snacks and starters, stuffed into bread and sometimes accompanied by a spicy tomato sauce or salsa. At home they make a perfect light lunch or addition to a barbecue.

Try making other popular Moroccan snacks, such as Cumin-spiced Chickpeas (page 26), which are traditionally sold in the evening in little paper cones. Briouats (fried pastries filled with lamb or tuna) are another tasty snack or a great start to a Moroccan feast.

< Beef Kefta Kebabs (page 12)

Beef Kefta Kebabs

MAKES 10

1 pound 10 ounces coarsely ground
beef

1 small onion, grated

2 tablespoons finely chopped fresh
flat-leaf parsley

2 tablespoons finely chopped fresh
cilantro

2 teaspoons paprika

2 teaspoons ground cumin

½ teaspoon cayenne pepper

½ teaspoon salt

¼ teaspoon freshly ground black
pepper

If using bamboo skewers, soak them in cold water for 30 minutes to prevent them
from burning. Alternatively, use metal skewers.

To make the keftas, place all the ingredients in a medium-sized bowl and mix
well to combine. Divide the mixture into 10 even-sized portions. Shape into oval
sausages and insert skewers through the center, pressing firmly to secure. Place
on a baking sheet and refrigerate for 1 hour or until firm.

Preheat barbecue grill to high.

Grill the keftas for 3–5 minutes on each side or until cooked to your liking.

Fish Kebabs

MAKES 8

1 pound 5 ounces hapuka or other firm white fish fillet (such as grouper, mahi mahi, orange roughy or snapper), cut into 1-inch cubes

CHERMOULA PASTE

3 cloves garlic, chopped

2 fresh hot red chili peppers, deseeded and chopped

½ bunch fresh cilantro, leaves chopped

½ bunch fresh flat-leaf parsley, leaves chopped

¼ cup olive oil

¼ cup freshly squeezed lemon juice

1½ teaspoons paprika

1 teaspoon ground cumin

1 teaspoon ground coriander

½ teaspoon freshly ground black pepper

½ teaspoon salt

To make the chermoula paste, place the garlic, chili peppers, cilantro and parsley in a food processor or blender and blend to a paste. Add the olive oil, lemon juice, spices and salt, and blend to combine. Mix the fish and chermoula in a large bowl and toss to coat. Cover and place in the refrigerator to marinate for at least 6 hours or overnight.

If using bamboo skewers, soak them in cold water for 30 minutes to prevent them from burning. Alternatively, use metal skewers.

Preheat barbecue grill to high. Thread fish onto skewers and grill for 2 minutes on each side, until cooked.

❇ Chermoula is a dry spice mix traditionally used to marinate fish and seafood.

Chicken Kebabs

MAKES 8

1 pound 5 ounces skinless chicken
   breast fillets

1½ tablespoons olive oil

juice of ½ lemon

¼ cup finely chopped fresh cilantro

2 cloves garlic, crushed

2 teaspoons paprika

1 teaspoon ground ginger

½ teaspoon ground turmeric

½ teaspoon salt

¼ teaspoon freshly ground black
   pepper

Trim the chicken of any excess fat and cut into 1-inch cubes.

Combine all of the ingredients in a medium-sized bowl and toss to coat. Cover and place in the refrigerator to marinate for at least 6 hours or overnight.

If using bamboo skewers, soak them in cold water for 30 minutes to prevent them from burning. Alternatively, use metal skewers.

Preheat barbecue grill to high.

Thread the chicken onto skewers and grill for 3–4 minutes on each side, until cooked.

Sardine Keftas

MAKES 16

2 pounds 3 ounces fresh sardines

2 tablespoons fine soft breadcrumbs

¼ cup olive oil

CHERMOULA PASTE

1 clove garlic, chopped

1 tablespoon finely chopped fresh cilantro

1 tablespoon finely chopped fresh flat-leaf parsley

1 tablespoon olive oil

1 tablespoon freshly squeezed lemon juice

1 teaspoon paprika

1 teaspoon ground cumin

1 teaspoon ground coriander

¼ teaspoon freshly ground black pepper

½ teaspoon salt

To make the chermoula paste, place the garlic, cilatro and parsley in a food processor or blender and blend to a paste. Add the olive oil, lemon juice, spices and salt, and blend to combine.

Clean the sardines, removing the heads, tails and bones. Coarsely chop the flesh and pass through a grater or mincer, or finely chop in a food processor or blender.

Combine the minced sardines, chermoula paste and breadcrumbs in a bowl. Shape into plum-sized balls and flatten to create patties.

Heat the olive oil in a large non-stick fry pan over medium heat. Cook the patties for 3 minutes on each side, until browned and cooked through.

Lamb Briouats

MAKES 20

2 tablespoons olive oil

1 medium-sized onion, grated

1 clove garlic, crushed

2 teaspoons ground cumin

2 teaspoons paprika

1 teaspoon ground cinnamon

½ teaspoon cayenne pepper

1 pound 2 ounces coarsely ground lamb

4 large eggs, lightly beaten, plus 1 egg yolk, lightly beaten

salt and freshly ground black pepper

10 spring roll wrappers

vegetable oil, for deep-frying

small piece of bread, to test vegetable oil

Heat the olive oil in a large fry pan over low–medium heat. Add the onion, garlic and spices, and cook until softened and fragrant. Add the ground lamb and cook, stirring occasionally, for 3–5 minutes, until browned and just cooked through. Add the 4 beaten eggs and cook, stirring, for an additional minute. Season with salt and freshly ground black pepper. Transfer to a medium-sized bowl and refrigerate for 30 minutes or until cooled.

Lay a spring roll wrapper on a clean counter top and cut in half lengthwise. Keep the remaining wrappers covered with food wrap to prevent them from drying out.

Place a spoonful of filling at the end of each spring roll wrapper and fold it back and forth in triangles to create a triangular bundle. Brush the edges with a little egg yolk and press to seal. Repeat the process with the remaining filling and spring roll wrappers.

Heat vegetable oil to 360°F in a large fry pan or until a small piece of bread browns in 15 seconds when tested.

Deep-fry the briouats in batches for 30–40 seconds on each side, until golden and crisp. Remove using a slotted spoon and drain on paper towels.

✳ In Morocco, briouats are traditionally made with warka pastry. Warka pastry is difficult and time consuming to make and near impossible to buy outside of Morocco. Spring-roll wrappers are the closest substitute.

Tuna Briouats

MAKES 4

1 (6½-ounce) can tuna, drained

1 preserved lemon, skin finely
chopped

½ small red onion, finely chopped

1 teaspoon cayenne pepper

2 tablespoons finely chopped fresh
flat-leaf parsley

1 tablespoon finely chopped fresh
cilantro

salt and freshly ground black pepper

cornstarch, for dusting

4 spring-roll wrappers

4 small eggs, plus 2 egg yolks

vegetable oil, for deep-frying

Combine the tuna with the preserved lemon, red onion, cayenne pepper, herbs and the seasoning in a medium-sized bowl. Lightly dust your work surface with cornstarch and lay a spring-roll wrapper on top. Cover remaining wrappers with food wrap to prevent drying out. Place one-quarter of the filling in the center of the wrapper. Make a well in the center of the filling and crack an egg into it. Fold two of the edges into the center, to cover the filling. Brush remaining edges with egg yolk and fold over to enclose the filling, pressing to seal. Repeat with remaining filling and wrappers.

Heat the vegetable oil to 360°F. As soon as assembled, deep-fry the briouats, in batches, for 20–30 seconds on each side. The egg yolk should still be runny in the center. Remove and drain on paper towels.

Moroccan Calzone

Rghaif

MAKES 10

olive oil, for frying

BEEF FILLING

2 tablespoons olive oil

1 medium-sized onion, finely chopped

2 tablespoons paprika

2 teaspoons ground cumin

1 teaspoon cayenne pepper

1 pound 2 ounces coarsley ground beef

water, to cook beef filling

salt and freshly ground black pepper

DOUGH

3 cups all-purpose flour

2 teaspoons salt

1 tablespoon dry yeast

2 teaspoons superfine sugar

1 cup lukewarm water

To make the beef filling, heat the olive oil in a large fry pan over low–medium heat. Add the onion and spices, and cook until softened and fragrant. Add the ground beef and cook for 3–4 minutes, stirring occasionally, until browned. Pour in ⅓ cup water and bring to a boil. Decrease the heat to low and gently simmer until the liquid has evaporated. Season with salt and freshly gound black pepper, and set aside to cool. >

To make the dough, combine the all-purpose flour, salt, yeast and superfine sugar in a medium-sized bowl. Gradually add the water, stirring, until a dough begins to form.

Knead the dough for 15–20 minutes, until it becomes a smooth elastic ball. With lightly oiled hands, shape the dough into 10 even-sized balls. Stretch and roll the dough out, one ball at a time, to make 8-inch paper-thin squares.

Spread one-tenth of the filling in the center of each square. Fold two opposite edges into the center, overlapping to cover the filling. Then fold the remaining edges in, again overlapping, to completely enclose the filling. Using your hands, flatten out the dough bundle to its original size. Transfer to a lightly oiled baking sheet and put in a warm place to rise for 30–45 minutes or until doubled in size.

Heat a medium-sized fry pan over medium–high heat. Drizzle with olive oil and cook the bundles, one or two at a time, for 1–2 minutes on each side or until golden brown.

Spiced Lentils

2 tablespoons olive oil

1 small red onion, finely chopped

2 cloves garlic, finely chopped

1 teaspoon ground cumin

1 teaspoon paprika

4 tomatoes, peeled, deseeded and finely chopped

2 cups dried green or brown lentils

½ cup water, to cook lentils

2 tablespoons finely chopped fresh flat-leaf parsley

2 tablespoons finely chopped fresh cilantro

salt and freshly ground black pepper

Heat the olive oil in a large fry pan over low–medium heat. Add the red onion, garlic, cumin and paprika and sauté until softened and fragrant.

Add the chopped tomatoes and cook for 3 minutes, until softened. Add the lentils and ½ cup water and bring to a boil. Reduce the heat to low and cook for 8–10 minutes, until tender.

Stir in the parsley, cilantro, and salt and freshly ground black pepper.

Cumin-spiced Chickpeas

SERVES 4

1½ cups dried chickpeas

cold water, to soak and cook chickpeas

2 tablespoons olive oil

1 tablespoon finely chopped fresh
   cilantro

1 tablespoon ground cumin

salt and freshly ground black pepper

Soak the chickpeas in cold water for at least 6 hours or overnight.

Drain and rinse the chickpeas, and place in a medium-sized saucepan. Cover with cold water and bring to a boil over high heat. Cook for 1 hour or until tender. Drain and set aside.

Heat the olive oil in a large fry pan over low heat. Add the chickpeas, cilantro and cumin and toss to coat. Season with salt and freshly ground black pepper. Drain on paper towels.

❋ These chickpeas are a typical street food, usually served in paper cones.

❋ Dried broad beans (fava) can be prepared in the same way.

Fried Potato Cakes

Maakouda

MAKES 10

3 medium-sized potatoes, washed

cold water, to cook potatoes

2 large eggs

2 tablespoons finely chopped fresh flat-leaf parsley

2 tablespoons finely chopped fresh cilantro

2 teaspoons ground cumin

1 teaspoon paprika

¼ teaspoon ground turmeric

salt and freshly ground black pepper

vegetable oil, for frying

¼ cup all-purpose flour

Place the unpeeled potatoes in a medium-sized saucepan and cover with cold water. Bring to a boil over high heat. Decrease the heat to medium and cook for 35–40 minutes, until tender. Drain and set aside to cool slightly. Peel the potatoes and mash or pass through a potato ricer or food mill.

Combine the potatoes with 1 egg and the herbs and spices in a bowl. Add salt and freshly ground black pepper. Shape into 10 even-sized balls and flatten to make patties.

Pour vegetable oil into a medium-sized fry pan to a depth of ¾-inch and place over medium heat.

Lightly beat the remaining egg in a shallow bowl and place the all-purpose flour in another. Dip the potato cakes into the egg, then lightly coat in flour. Cook for 2–3 minutes on each side, until golden brown. Drain on paper towels.

Soups & Salads

Soup, although generally not common in Morocco, plays a significant role in the Muslim month of Ramadan. During this festival, bowls of harira, considered to be the national soup, are made in endless variations and served at every family table at sundown to break the day's fast. A rich, nutritious soup filled with vegetables and legumes, harira is traditionally served alongside fresh dates, mounds of toasted slelou (sesame, almond and honey paste) and sweet, sticky pastries such as chebbakia (sesame cookies) and almond-filled briouats.

Most Moroccan meals begin with or are accompanied by an array of salads. These range from simple raw salads of orange and lettuce, or the popular Moroccan salad of tomato, cucumber and red onion, to slow-cooked bakkoula (mallow) or spicy cauliflower salad.

‹ Harira Soup (page 32)

Harira Soup

SERVES 8

1 pound lamb shoulder chops

3 tablespoons butter

2 large onions, finely chopped

1 teaspoon ground turmeric

1 teaspoon freshly ground black
  pepper

½ teaspoon ground cinnamon

pinch of saffron threads, crushed

wings, neck, heart and liver
  of 1 chicken

1 cup finely chopped celery leaves

1 pound 9 ounces tomato puree

¾ cup dried green or brown lentils

2 tablespoons tomato paste

¾-quart water, to cook lentils

2 tablespoons all-purpose flour

small handful of vermicelli pasta

½ cup finely chopped fresh cilantro

½ cup finely chopped fresh
  flat-leaf parsley

juice of 1 lemon

salt

Remove the lamb from the bones and cut the meat into ⅝-inch cubes. Set the meat and bones aside.

Melt the butter in a large saucepan over low–medium heat. Add the onions and spices, and sauté until softened and fragrant. Add the lamb and bones, chicken pieces and celery leaves, and cook, stirring occasionally, for 15 minutes. Add the tomato puree, lentils and tomato paste and stir together. Pour in ¾-quart water and bring to a boil. Decrease the heat to low and cook for 30–40 minutes, until the lentils are tender.

Combine the all-purpose flour with the remaining water in a small bowl. Gradually pour the flour mixture into the hot soup, stirring continuously to prevent lumps. Gently simmer for 5 minutes.

Increase the heat and bring to a boil. Add the vermicelli pasta, cilantro, parsley and lemon juice. Cook, stirring occasionally, for 5–10 minutes, until the pasta is cooked. Season with salt.

✳ Harira is Morocco's most well-known soup. A highly nutritious soup with endless variations, it is eaten at sundown to break the fast throughout the month of Ramadan. It is traditionally served with dates, hard-boiled eggs and sweet pastries such as chebbakia (page 179) or almond briouats (page 182).

Broad Bean (Fava) Soup

Beyssara

SERVES 6

1 pound dried broad (fava) beans

¾-quart vegetable stock or water

5 cloves garlic, peeled

1½ teaspoons paprika, plus extra to garnish

1½ teaspoons ground cumin, plus extra to garnish

salt

drizzle of extra-virgin olive oil

Soak the fava beans in cold water overnight. Drain, rinse and skin the fava beans.

Place the fava beans, vegetable stock or water, garlic, paprika and cumin in a medium-sized saucepan and bring to a boil. (Do not add the salt at this stage as it will cause the fava beans to toughen.) Decrease the heat to low–medium and simmer for 1–1½ hours, until the fava beans are soft.

Purée the fava beans, the garlic and the cooking liquid together using a hand-held blender or food processor. Add a little more liquid if the mixture is too thick. Season with salt.

To serve, ladle the soup into bowls, drizzle with extra-vigin olive oil and sprinkle with paprika and cumin.

Aniseed & Semolina Soup

SERVES 8

¾-quart water, to cook semolina

1½ cups coarse semolina

2 tablespoons butter

pinch of saffron threads, crushed

3 cups milk

2 teaspoons ground aniseed

salt and freshly ground black pepper

Place ¾-quart water in a medium-sized saucepan over medium–high heat until hot, not boiling. Pour in the semolina in a thin stream, stirring to prevent lumps. Add the butter and saffron, and bring to a boil. Decrease the heat to low and cook for 20–30 minutes, until the semolina is soft, swollen and cooked.

Heat the milk and ground aniseed together over low–medium heat, until almost simmering. Add to the semolina and stir to combine. Season with salt and freshly ground black pepper.

✻ Semolina is coarse grains of durum wheat.

Caraway Soup

SERVES 8

¾-quart milk

¾-quart water, to heat with milk

4 ounces all-purpose flour

2 cups water, to combine with flour

2 tablespoons ground caraway seeds

6–8 sprigs fresh mint

¼ cup freshly squeezed lemon juice

salt

Heat the milk together with ¾-quart water in a medium-sized saucepan over medium–high heat until hot, not boiling. Combine the all-purpose flour with 2 cups water in a medium-sized bowl. Gradually pour the flour mixture into the hot milk and water, whisking to prevent lumps.

Add the caraway and mint, and bring to a boil, stirring constantly. Decrease the heat to low and gently simmer for 5 minutes. Remove from the heat and set aside for 30 minutes to allow the flavors to infuse.

Strain the soup through a fine-mesh sieve to remove any lumps. Discard the mint.

Return the soup to the heat and gently bring to just below the simmering point. Add the lemon juice, stirring to combine, and season with salt.

❋ This soup is traditionally served with steamed sheep's head.

Beet Salad

SERVES 4

4 medium-sized beets

water, to cover and cook beets

1½ tablespoons olive oil

1 tablespoon freshly squeezed lemon
   juice

½ teaspoon ground cumin

salt

2 tablespoons finely chopped fresh
   cilantro

Trim the stems off the beets and wash thoroughly. Place in a large saucepan, cover with water and bring to a boil over medium–high heat. Cook for 1 hour or until tender. Let set in the water to cool for 30 minutes.

Wearing food-handling gloves (to prevent staining your hands), peel the beets. Cut into bite-sized pieces and place in a medium-sized bowl.

Combine the olive oil, lemon juice and cumin in a small bowl. Pour the dressing over the beets and stir to coat. Season with salt and set aside for 1 hour to allow the flavors to develop.

Sprinkle with the fresh cilantro and serve.

Spicy Potato Salad

SERVES 4

¼ cup olive oil

2 teaspoons paprika

2 teaspoons ground cumin

4 medium-sized potatoes, cut into
¾-inch cubes

⅓ cup of water, to cook potatoes

2 tablespoons finely chopped fresh
flat-leaf parsley

2 tablespoons finely chopped fresh
cilantro

salt and freshly ground black pepper

Heat the olive oil in a large fry pan over medium heat. Add the spices and potatoes, and cook for 3–5 minutes, stirring occasionally, until golden.

Add ⅓ cup water, then cover and cook over low heat for 10–15 minutes, until tender. Stir in the parsley, cilantro, and salt and freshly ground black pepper.

Serve warm.

Potato & Bell Pepper Salad

SERVES 4

2 tablespoons olive oil

2 cloves garlic, finely chopped

1 teaspoon ground turmeric

1 teaspoon paprika

½ teaspoon ground ginger

2 tomatoes, peeled, deseeded and
coarsely chopped

2 green bell peppers, deseeded and
coarsely chopped

3 tablespoons finely chopped fresh
cilantro

$^1/_3$ cup water

2 large potatoes, cut into ¾-inch
cubes

1 preserved lemon, deseeded and
coarsely chopped

salt and freshly ground black pepper

Heat the olive oil in a large fry pan over low heat. Add the garlic and spices, and
sauté until softened and fragrant. Add the tomatoes, green bell peppers, cilantro
and water. Cover and cook for 45 minutes.

Add the potatoes and preserved lemon to the pan, cover and cook for an additional 15 minutes. Uncover and cook for 20 minutes, stirring occasionally, until the
liquid has evaporated and the potatoes are tender. Season with salt and freshly
ground black pepper.

Serve warm or cold.

Sweet Carrot & Orange Salad

SERVES 4

2 oranges, peeled

6 medium-sized carrots, grated

juice of ½ lemon

1 teaspoon orange-blossom water

2 tablespoons granulated white sugar

1½ teaspoons ground cinnamon, plus
   extra for dusting

pinch of salt

Using a small, sharp knife and working with a bowl underneath to catch any juice, cut the flesh out of each orange segment and place in a separate medium-sized bowl. Squeeze any remaining juice from the oranges into the bowl.

Add the grated carrots to the bowl with the orange segments.

Combine the reserved orange juice with the lemon juice, orange-blossom water, granulated white sugar, cinnamon and salt in a bowl. Pour the dressing over the salad and stir to combine. Refrigerate for 1 hour to allow the flavors to develop.

Serve chilled, dusted with cinnamon.

✳ Orange-blossom water, also known as orange-flower water, is a solution of orange-blossom oil in water. Orange extract, orange-flavored liqueur or orange zest may be substitued.

Cucumber Salad

SERVES 4

6 English (seedless) cucumbers,
   peeled and deseeded

3 tablespoons olive oil

2 tablespoons white-wine vinegar

1 tablespoon superfine sugar

1 tablespoon finely chopped fresh
   thyme

salt

Coarsely grate the cucumber and drain off any excess liquid.

Combine the olive oil, white-wine vinegar, superfine sugar and thyme in a small bowl. Add the grated cucumber and stir to combine. Season with salt and refrigerate until chilled.

Marshmallow Leaf Salad

Bakkoula

SERVES 4

6 cups finely chopped spinach ✻

1 cup finely chopped fresh
    flat-leaf parsley

¼ cup finely chopped fresh cilantro

4 cloves garlic, peeled

2 teaspoons salt

2 teaspoons paprika

water, to cover and cook spinach

¼ cup olive oil

¼ cup lemon juice

1½ teaspoons ground cumin

¼ cup green olives, to garnish

1 preserved lemon, quartered, flesh
    discarded and skin finely sliced, to
    garnish

Place the spinach, parsley, cilantro, garlic, salt and paprika in a large saucepan. Add ½ cup water, cover and cook over low heat for 10 minutes, until tender. Add ¼ cup water, stir, cover and cook for an additional 2 hours.

Add the olive oil and cook, uncovered, for 20 minutes or until all the liquid has evaporated. Add the lemon juice and cumin, stir to combine and cook for an additional 10–15 minutes, until all the liquid has evaporated. Transfer to a medium-sized bowl and refrigerate until chilled.

Serve garnished with olives and slices of preserved lemon.

✻ Marshmallow leaves can be difficult to find outside of Morocco. Here, spinach is used as a substitute.

Orange & Lettuce Salad

SERVES 4

2 oranges

2 baby cos (or Romaine) lettuces

2 tablespoons lemon juice

1 teaspoon orange-blossom water

1 tablespoon olive oil

2 teaspoons superfine sugar

pinch of salt

Using a small, sharp knife, cut the flesh out of each orange segment and place in a medium-sized bowl.

Roughly tear the lettuce into small pieces and add to the bowl with the orange segments.

Combine the lemon juice, orange-blossom water, olive oil, superfine sugar and salt in a small bowl. Pour the dressing over the salad and toss to combine.

Moroccan Salad

SERVES 4

3 tomatoes, peeled, deseeded and
    finely diced

1 English (seedless) cucumber, peeled
    and finely diced

2 green bell peppers, finely diced

1 small red onion, finely diced

2 tablespoons olive oil

juice of ½ lemon

salt and freshly ground black pepper

Place the tomatoes, cucumber, green bell peppers and red onion in a medium-sized bowl.

Mix the olive oil and lemon juice in a small bowl. Add to the vegetables and stir to combine. Season with salt and freshly ground black pepper.

Spicy Cauliflower Salad

SERVES 4

1 cauliflower, cut into large florets

water, to cover and cook cauliflower

2 tablespoons olive oil

2 cloves garlic, finely chopped

1 teaspoon ground turmeric

1 teaspoon paprika

2 tomatoes, peeled, deseeded and
coarsely chopped

3 tablespoons finely chopped fresh
cilantro

water, to simmer

¼ cup green olives

1 preserved lemon, deseeded and
coarsely chopped

salt and freshly ground black pepper

Place the cauliflower florets in a medium-sized saucepan and cover with water. Place over medium–high heat and bring to a boil. Decrease the heat to low and cook for 2 minutes, then drain and set aside.

Heat the olive oil in a large fry pan over low heat. Add the garlic, turmeric and paprika and sauté until softened and fragrant. Add the tomatoes, cilantro and ⅓ cup water. Cover and simmer for 30 minutes.

Add the cauliflower florets, green olives and preserved lemon and cook for an additional 20 minutes, stirring occasionally, until the liquid has evaporated and the cauliflower florets are tender. Season with salt and freshly ground black pepper.

Serve warm or cold.

Couscous

In Morocco, couscous refers not only to the swollen semolina grains but to the flavorsome stew and broth over which the granules are steamed. This combination creates one of Morocco's most famous dishes. Traditionally served on Friday, the main day of prayer, couscous is ever-present as the final course in celebratory feasts.

Packaged couscous is readily available in supermarkets, and is quick and easy to prepare. However, instant couscous cannot compare with the more time-consuming Moroccan dish. Fluffy and infused with the succulent flavors of meat, spices and vegetables, traditional Moroccan couscous is an absolute delight.

‹ Traditional Moroccan Couscous (page 54)

Traditional Moroccan Couscous

SERVES 6

3 cups couscous

1 tablespoon salt

water, to separate grains

2 tablespoons olive oil

Step 1. Place the couscous in a large, deep baking pan. Mix the salt together with 1 quart 2 ounces (34 fluid ounces) water in a large bowl. Sprinkle 1½ cups of the salted water over the couscous, rubbing it through with your fingers to separate the grains. Set aside for 15 minutes to allow the grains to swell and dry out a little.

Step 2. Rub your fingers through the couscous again, breaking up any lumps. Place the couscous in the top of a steamer saucepan lined with cheese cloth and place over the simmering stew (see following recipes), making sure that the steamer is not touching the liquid below. Cover and cook until steam begins to rise through the couscous, then cook for an additional 10 minutes. Place the couscous into a large, deep baking pan, sifting through the grains with your fingers or a spoon, and set aside to dry out a little. Gradually sprinkle with 1 cup water, rubbing it through with your fingers and separating the grains. Drizzle with the olive oil and toss through to coat. Set aside for 15 minutes, to allow the grains to swell and dry out a little.

Step 3. Repeat the steaming, drying and sifting process, then sprinkle couscous with another 1 cup water. Set aside for 15 minutes to allow the grains to swell and dry out a little or, if preparing the couscous in advance, cover with a clean, damp cloth and set aside until required. The couscous can be kept at this stage for 3–4 hours.

Step 4. Rub your fingers through the couscous again, separating the grains and breaking up any lumps. Gradually sprinkle with the remaining water, rubbing it through with your fingers. Set aside for 15 minutes to allow the grains to swell and dry out a little. Place the couscous in the top of the steamer and steam for the third and final time over the simmering stew, or if the stew has finished cooking, steam over a saucepan of boiling water. Place the couscous into a large, deep baking pan. Smooth the grains out flat, allowing the steam to rise and the couscous to dry out a little.

Serve with the accompanying stew and broth.

✳ If time is short, use instant couscous (available at supermarkets) and prepare it following the directions on the package.

Seven-vegetable Couscous

SERVES 6

1 recipe traditional Moroccan couscous
(page 54)

1 pound 2 ounces to 1 pound
7 ounces lamb shanks

¼ cup olive oil

¼ cup vegetable oil

6 medium-sized tomatoes, peeled

1 large red onion, sliced

1 tablespoon salt

2 teaspoons paprika

1½ teaspoons freshly ground black
pepper

1½ teaspoons ground turmeric

1½ teaspoons ground ginger

½ bunch fresh cilantro, washed and
tied with kitchen string

water, to cover lamb

1 beef bouillon cube

4 medium-sized carrots, cut in half
across, then in half lengthwise and
cored

2–3 medium-sized turnips, quartered

2–3 medium-sized potatoes, cut in
half lengthwise

4 medium-sized zucchini, cut in half
across, then in half lengthwise and
deseeded

¼ small pumpkin, cut into large
chunks

1 fresh mild green chili pepper

Prepare the couscous using the traditional method or use instant couscous and
follow the directions on the package.

Place the lamb shanks, olive and vegetable oils, 1 coarsely chopped tomato, the
red onion, salt, spices and cilantro in the bottom of a large steamer saucepan.

Cook over medium–high heat for 5–10 minutes, until the lamb shanks are browned and the spices are fragrant.

Pour in enough water to just cover the lamb shanks. Crumble in the bouillon cube, cover the pan and bring to a boil over high heat. Decrease the heat to low–medium, cover and simmer gently for 1 hour.

Cut the remaining tomatoes in half, remove and discard the seeds, and chop coarsely. Add the tomatoes, carrots, turnips and potatoes to the saucepan with the lamb shanks and continue to simmer gently for 30 minutes.

Add the remaining vegetables and the green chili pepper to the pan and simmer for an additional 30 minutes, adding a little more water if necessary.

Pile the couscous onto a large serving plate, making a slight well in the center. Arrange the vegetables around the outside of the couscous and spoon the stew into the center, drizzling a little of the broth over the top. Place any remaining broth in a bowl, to be spooned over the couscous as desired.

Couscous with Veal & Raisins

SERVES 6

1 recipe traditional Moroccan couscous
(page 54)

2 tablespoons vegetable oil

7 tablespoons (3½ ounces) butter

1 pound 2 ounces veal osso bucco

2 teaspoons ground cinnamon

1 teaspoon ground ginger

½ teaspoon ground turmeric

½ teaspoon ground cumin

pinch of saffron threads

½ teaspoon freshly ground black
pepper

1 teaspoon salt

water, to cover veal

½ bunch fresh flat-leaf parsley,
washed and tied with kitchen string

4 large red onions,
thickly sliced

2 cloves garlic, finely chopped

3 tablespoons honey

1 cup raisins

water, to thin broth

Prepare the couscous using the traditional method or use instant couscous and follow the directions on the package.

Heat the vegetable oil and half of the butter in the bottom of a large steamer saucepan. Add the veal osso bucco, spices and salt, and cook over medium–high heat for 5–10 minutes, until the veal is browned and the spices are fragrant. Pour in enough water to just cover the veal. Cover the pan and bring to a boil over high heat. Decrease the heat to low–medium, add the parsley, cover and simmer gently for 1½ hours. ❯

Melt the remaining butter in a separate medium-sized saucepan. Add the red onion and garlic, and sauté over low–medium heat for 20 minutes or until golden brown. Add the honey and raisins, and cook, stirring, for an additional 5–10 minutes, until sticky like jam.

Remove the veal osso bucco from the broth, then cut the meat into smaller chunks and return to the broth. Discard the bones. Add the onion mixture and additional water, if required. Continue to simmer gently for an additional 30 minutes.

Pile the couscous onto a large serving plate, making a slight well in the center. Place the veal osso bucco in the center, spoon over the onions and raisins and a little of the broth. Place any remaining broth in a bowl, to be spooned over the couscous as desired.

❋ Veal osso bucco is sliced veal knuckle or shin bone

Medfoun Couscous

SERVES 6

1 recipe traditional Moroccan couscous
   (page 54)

8 tablespoons butter

1 pound 2 ounces lamb shoulder or
   leg, cut into small chunks

2 large red onions, coarsely chopped

1 clove garlic, finely chopped

1 teaspoon ground cinnamon, plus
   extra to garnish

pinch of saffron threads, crumbled

½ teaspoon freshly ground black
   pepper

1 teaspoon salt

water, to cover lamb

confectioner's (powdered) sugar, to
   garnish

fresh milk, to serve

Prepare the couscous using the traditional method or use instant couscous and follow the directions on the package.

Heat the butter in the bottom of a large steamer saucepan. Add the lamb, red onions, garlic, spices and seasonings, and cook over medium–high heat for 5–10 minutes, until the lamb is browned and the spices are fragrant.

Pour in enough water to just cover the lamb, then cover the pan and bring to a boil. Decrease the heat to low–medium, cover and simmer gently for approximately 2 hours, stirring occasionally, until the stew is thick and the lamb is tender. **>**

Spread half of the couscous onto a large serving plate. Spoon the lamb stew over the top. Cover with the remaining couscous, creating a dome making sure the lamb is completely covered. Decorate with cinnamon and confectioner's sugar, creating alternate lines coming down from the top.

Serve with a drink of fresh milk, if desired.

❋ Medfouna means "buried". This dish is also known as 'lucky' or 'surprise' couscous because the piled-up couscous conceals the stew underneath.

Couscous with Chicken & Chickpeas

SERVES 6

1 recipe traditional Moroccan couscous
(page 54)

¼ cup vegetable oil

2 tablespoons butter

1 (3-pound 5-ounce) chicken,
quartered

2 large red onions, sliced

2 teaspoons ground turmeric

1½ teaspoons paprika

1 teaspoon ground ginger

1 teaspoon ground cinnamon

1 teaspoon ground cumin

½ teaspoon freshly ground black
pepper

pinch of saffron threads, crushed

1 teaspoon salt

water, to cover chicken

½ bunch fresh cilantro, washed and
tied with kitchen string

1½ tablespoons tomato paste

1 chicken bouillon cube

4 medium-sized carrots, cut in half
across, then in half lengthwise and
cored

¼ medium-sized pumpkin, coarsely
grated

4 medium-sized tomatoes, peeled,
deseeded and coarsely chopped

1 (10½-ounce) can chickpeas, drained
and rinsed

water, to thin stew

Prepare the couscous using the traditional method or use instant couscous and
follow the directions on the package. ❯

Heat the vegetable oil and butter in the bottom of a large steamer saucepan. Add the chicken pieces, red onions, spices and salt, and cook over medium–high heat for 5–10 minutes, until the chicken pieces are browned and the spices are fragrant.

Pour in enough water to just cover the chicken pieces, then add the cilantro, tomato paste and crumbled bouillon cube and bring to a boil. Decrease the heat to low–medium and gently simmer for 30 minutes.

Add the prepared vegetables to the stew and continue to simmer gently for an additional 30 minutes. Add the chickpeas and additional water, if required, and continue to simmer gently for an additional 20 minutes.

Pile the couscous onto a large serving plate, making a slight well in the center. Place the chicken pieces in the center, then spoon on the vegetables and a little of the broth. Place any remaining broth in a bowl, to be spooned over the couscous as desired.

Fish Couscous

SERVES 6

1 recipe traditional Moroccan couscous
(page 54)

¼ cup olive oil

1 large red onion, thickly sliced

2 cloves garlic, finely chopped

2 fresh hot red chili peppers, deseeded
and finely chopped

1½ teaspoons paprika

1 teaspoon ground cumin

1 teaspoon ground coriander

½ teaspoon freshly ground black
pepper

¼ teaspoon cayenne pepper

1 teaspoon salt

½ bunch fresh cilantro, washed

½ bunch fresh flat-leaf parsley,
washed

4 medium-sized carrots, cut in half
across, then in half lengthwise and
cored

4 medium-sized tomatoes, peeled,
deseeded and quartered

water, to cover vegetables

1 red bell pepper, sliced lengthwise

1 green bell pepper, sliced lengthwise

2 pounds 12 ounces snapper or other
firm white fish fillets, cut into
2-inch thick steaks

Prepare the couscous using the traditional method or use instant couscous and
follow the directions on the package. ❯

Heat the olive oil in the bottom of a large steamer saucepan. Add the red onion, garlic, red chili peppers, spices and salt, and cook over low–medium heat for 5–10 minutes, until softened and fragrant.

Tie the cilantro and parsley together using kitchen string. Add to the saucepan with the carrots and tomatoes. Pour in enough water to just cover the vegetables and bring to a boil. Decrease the heat to low–medium and simmer gently for 30 minutes. Add the red and green bell peppers to the stew and cook for an additional 30 minutes.

Add the fish to the stew and cook for 10–15 minutes, until the fish is cooked and the flesh flakes easily.

Pile the couscous onto a large serving plate, making a slight well in the center. Place the fish and vegetables in the well and drizzle with a little of the broth. Place any remaining broth in a bowl, to be spooned over the couscous as desired.

Tagines

The tagine is one of Morocco's most well-known dishes and it is very easy to prepare at home. There are many delicious combinations and flavorings. Try the M'qualli Chicken Tagine with Preserved Lemons and Olives (page 94) or a vegetarian dish made with spiced pumpkin and lentils (page 119).

The word 'tagine' applies not only to the meal, but also to the unique cooking vessel in which it is cooked. Tagine cookware is designed especially for slow cooking and has either a domed or conical lid. Steam rises inside to the top of the lid, condenses into liquid and runs down the sides back into the stew cooking below, keeping it moist and creating a flavorsome broth at the same time.

‹ Beef Kefta & Tomato Tagine (page 72)

Beef Kefta & Tomato Tagine

SERVES 4

2 tablespoons olive oil

1 medium-sized red onion, finely chopped

2 cloves garlic, finely chopped

2 teaspoons granulated white sugar

1 teaspoon ground cumin

1 teaspoon paprika

½ teaspoon cayenne pepper

8 medium-sized tomatoes, peeled, deseeded and coarsely chopped

water, to boil tomato mixture

salt and freshly ground black pepper

2 tablespoons finely chopped fresh flat-leaf parsley

BEEF KEFTAS

1 pound 5 ounces coarsely ground beef

1 small red onion, grated

2 tablespoons finely chopped fresh flat-leaf parsley

2 tablespoons finely chopped fresh cilantro

1 teaspoon paprika

1 teaspoon ground cumin

½ teaspoon cayenne pepper

¼ teaspoon freshly ground black pepper

½ teaspoon salt

2 tablespoons olive oil

Moroccan bread, to serve (page 225)

Heat the olive oil in a large fry pan over low–medium heat. Add the red onion, garlic, sugar and spices, and sauté until golden. Add the tomatoes and cook for 5 minutes, until softened. Pour in ⅓ cup water and bring to a boil.

Decrease the heat to low and cook for 10–15 minutes, until the mixture has a sauce-like consistency. Add salt and freshly ground black pepper.

To make the keftas, combine the coarsely ground beef, red onion, parsley, cilantro, spices and salt in a bowl. Shape into compact, walnut-sized balls.

Heat the olive oil in a large fry pan over medium–high heat. Cook the keftas in batches for 3–4 minutes, until browned all over.

Spoon half of the tomato sauce over the bottom of a medium–large tagine or heavy-based saucepan. Arrange the keftas on top. Spoon on the remaining tomato sauce and sprinkle with the parsley. Cover and cook over low–medium heat for 10–15 minutes, until the keftas are cooked through.

Serve with Moroccan bread (page 225).

Beef & Apple Tagine

SERVES 4

¼ cup olive oil

2 pounds 3 ounces stewing beef
(from brisket, chuck, plate or rib),
trimmed and cut into large 2-inch
chunks

1 large red onion, sliced

1 teaspoon ground ginger

½ teaspoon salt

¼ teaspoon freshly ground black
pepper

pinch of saffron threads

1½ cups beef stock or water

2 tablespoons butter

2 tablespoons honey

3 medium-sized cooking apples,
quartered and cored

1 teaspoon ground cinnamon

2 tablespoons finely chopped fresh
cilantro

Heat the olive oil in a medium–large tagine or heavy-based saucepan over medium heat. Add the stewing beef, red onion, ginger, salt, freshly ground black pepper and saffron, and cook for 5–10 minutes, stirring occasionally, until the stewing beef is browned and the spices are fragrant. Pour in 1¼ cups beef stock or water and bring to a boil. Reduce the heat to low, cover and cook for 1½ hours.

Melt the butter and honey in a medium-sized saucepan over low heat. Add the apples and cinnamon, cover and cook for 10–15 minutes, until almost tender. Arrange apple quarters around the stewing beef in the tagine. Add the remaining beef stock or water and sprinkle with the cilantro. Cover and cook for 30 minutes, or until the meat and apples are tender.

Beef & Sweet Potato Tagine

SERVES 4

¼ cup olive oil

2 pounds 3 ounces stewing beef, trimmed and cut into 2-inch chunks

1 large red onion, sliced into rounds

2 cloves garlic, finely chopped

1 teaspoon paprika

1 teaspoon ground ginger

½ teaspoon cayenne pepper

½ teaspoon ground cumin

¼ teaspoon ground turmeric

¼ teaspoon freshly ground black pepper

½ teaspoon salt

1½ cups beef or vegetable stock, or water

1 large sweet potato, sliced into ³/₈-inch thick rounds

1 tablespoon finely chopped fresh flat-leaf parsley

1 tablespoon finely chopped fresh cilantro

Heat the olive oil in a medium–large tagine or heavy-based saucepan over medium heat. Add the stewing beef, red onion, garlic, spices and salt, and cook for 5–10 minutes, stirring occasionally, until the stewing beef is browned and the spices are fragrant. Pour in 1¼ cups of the beef or vegetable stock or water and bring to a boil. Reduce the heat to low, cover and cook for 1½ hours.

Arrange the sweet potato around the stewing beef and pour in the remaining beef or vegetable stock or water. Sprinkle with the parsley and cilantro. Cover and cook for an additional 30 minutes, until the meat and sweet potato are tender.

Veal & Quince Tagine

SERVES 4

¼ cup olive oil

2¾ pounds veal osso bucco

1 large red onion, sliced

1½ teaspoons ground ginger

½ teaspoon salt

¼ teaspoon freshly ground black
pepper

pinch of saffron threads

1½ cups chicken or vegetable stock,
or water

2 tablespoons butter

2 tablespoons honey

2 quinces, quartered and cored

1 teaspoon ground cinnamon

2 tablespoons finely chopped fresh
flat-leaf parsley

Heat the olive oil in a medium–large tagine or heavy-based saucepan over medium heat. Add the veal osso bucco, red onion, ginger, salt, freshly ground black pepper and saffron, and cook for 5–10 minutes, stirring occasionally, until the veal osso bucco is browned and the spices are fragrant. Pour in 1¼ cups chicken or vegetable stock or water and bring to a boil. Reduce the heat to low, cover and cook for 1½ hours.

Melt the butter and honey together in a medium saucepan over low heat. Add the quinces and cinnamon and cook for 20–30 minutes. Transfer the quinces to the tagine, arranging them around the veal osso bucco. Add the remaining stock or water and sprinkle with the parsley. Cover and cook for an additional 30 minutes, until the meat and quinces are tender.

Veal, Pea & Artichoke Tagine

SERVES 4

¼ cup olive oil

2¾ pounds veal osso bucco

2 large red onions, finely chopped

3 cloves garlic, finely chopped

1 teaspoon ground ginger

½ teaspoon ground turmeric

¼ teaspoon freshly ground black pepper

pinch of saffron threads

½ teaspoon salt

1½ cups chicken or vegetable stock, or water

8 small artichokes

water, to submerge artichoke hearts

juice of ½ lemon

1½ cups freshly shelled or frozen peas

2 tablespoons finely chopped fresh cilantro

Heat olive oil in a large tagine or heavy-based saucepan over medium heat. Add veal osso bucco, red onion, garlic, spices and salt, and cook for 5–10 minutes, stirring occasionally, until the veal is browned. Add 1¼ cups chicken or vegetable stock or water and bring to a boil. Reduce heat to low, cover and cook for 1½ hours.

Discard the artichoke leaves, scoop out the chokes and cut off the stalks. Submerge the artichoke hearts in a bowl of cold water with the lemon juice added for 10 minutes. Arrange the artichoke hearts around the veal osso bucco. Pour in the remaining stock chicken or vegetable or water, cover and cook for an additional 20 minutes, until the meat and artichoke hearts are tender. Add the peas and cilantro and cook for 10 minutes.

Veal Tagine with Parsley, Preserved Lemons & Olives

SERVES 4

¼ cup olive oil

2¾ pounds veal osso bucco

2 large red onions, grated

2 cloves garlic, finely chopped

1½ teaspoons ground ginger

1½ teaspoons ground paprika

½ teaspoon ground cinnamon

¼ teaspoon freshly ground black pepper

pinch of saffron threads

½ teaspoon salt

1½ cups chicken stock or water

1½ preserved lemons, quartered, flesh discarded and skin thickly sliced

1½ cups finely chopped fresh flat-leaf parsley

⅓ cup green olives

juice of ½ lemon

Moroccan bread, to serve (page 225)

Heat the olive oil in a medium–large tagine or heavy-based saucepan over medium heat. Add the veal osso bucco, red onions, garlic, spices and salt, and cook for 5–10 minutes, stirring occasionally, until the veal osso bucco is browned and the spices are fragrant. Pour in 1¼ cups of the chicken stock or water and bring to a boil. Reduce the heat to low, cover and cook for 1½ hours.

Arrange the preserved lemons around the meat. Scatter with the parsley and green olives, then pour in the remaining chicken stock or water and the lemon juice. Cover and cook for an additional 30 minutes, or until the meat is tender.

Serve with Moroccan bread (page 225).

Veal, Green Bean
& Tomato Tagine

SERVES 4

¼ cup olive oil

2¾ pounds veal osso bucco

1 large onion, sliced

2 cloves garlic, finely chopped

1 tablespoon paprika

1 teaspoon ground ginger

½ teaspoon ground turmeric

¼ teaspoon freshly ground black
   pepper

pinch of saffron threads

½ teaspoon salt

6 tomatoes, peeled, deseeded and
   chopped

1½ cups chicken or vegetable stock,
   or water

juice of ½ lemon

1 pound green beans, trimmed

Moroccan bread, to serve (page 225)

Heat the olive oil in a medium–large tagine or heavy-based saucepan over medium heat. Add the veal osso bucco, onion, garlic, spices and salt and cook for 5–10 minutes, stirring occasionally, until the veal oso bucco is browned and the spices are fragrant. Add the tomatoes, then pour in 1¼ cups chicken or vegetable stock or water and bring to a boil. Reduce heat to low, cover and cook for 1½ hours.

Pour in the remaining chicken or vegetable stock or water and the lemon juice. Scatter the green beans around the outside of the veal osso bucco. Cover and cook for an additional 30 minutes, or until the meat and green beans are tender.

Serve with Moroccan bread (page 225).

Veal & Cauliflower Tagine

SERVES 4

¼ cup olive oil

2¾ pounds veal osso bucco

1 large onion, finely chopped

2 cloves garlic, finely chopped

1½ teaspoons ground cumin

1 teaspoon ground ginger

½ teaspoon ground turmeric

¼ teaspoon freshly ground black
   pepper

pinch of saffron threads

½ teaspoon salt

1½ cups chicken stock or water

1 cauliflower, cut into florets

juice of ½ lemon

2 tomatoes, peeled, deseeded and
   coarsely chopped

2 tablespoons finely chopped fresh
   cilantro

Moroccan bread, to serve (page 225)

Heat the olive oil in a medium–large tagine or heavy-based saucepan over medium heat. Add the veal osso bucco, onion, garlic, spices and salt, and cook for 5–10 minutes, stirring occasionally, until the veal osso bucco is browned and the spices are fragrant. Pour in 1¼ cups chicken stock or water and bring to a boil. Reduce the heat to low, cover and cook for 1¼ hours.

Arrange cauliflower florets around the veal osso bucco. Pour in remaining chicken stock or water and lemon juice. Scatter tomatoes in the center and sprinkle with cilantro. Cover and cook for 30–45 minutes, until the meat and cauliflower florets are tender.

Serve with Moroccan bread (page 225).

Lamb & Prune Tagine

SERVES 4

¼ cup olive oil

2 pounds 3 ounces boneless lamb
   shoulder or leg, trimmed and cut in
   2-inch chunks

2 large red onions, sliced

1½ teaspoons ground cinnamon

1½ teaspoons ground ginger

1 teaspoon ground cumin

¼ teaspoon freshly ground black
   pepper

pinch of saffron threads

½ teaspoon salt

1½ cups chicken or vegetable stock,
   or water

1½ cups pitted prunes

2 teaspoons sesame seeds, toasted

Moroccan bread, to serve (page 225)

Heat the olive oil in a medium–large tagine or heavy-based saucepan over medium heat. Add the lamb, red onions, spices and salt, and cook for 5–10 minutes, stirring occasionally, until the lamb is browned and the spices fragrant. Pour in 1¼ cups of the chicken or vegetable stock or water and bring to a boil. Reduce the heat to low, cover and cook for 1½ hours.

Pour in the remaining chicken or vegetable stock or water and scatter with the pitted prunes. Cover and cook for an additional 30 minutes, until the meat is tender. Sprinkle with the toasted sesame seeds.

Serve with Moroccan bread (page 225).

Lamb & Fennel Tagine

SERVES 4

¼ cup olive oil

2¾ pounds lamb loin chops

1 large red onion, sliced

2 cloves garlic, finely chopped

1½ teaspoons ground ginger

½ teaspoon ground turmeric

¼ teaspoon freshly ground black
  pepper

pinch of saffron threads

½ teaspoon salt

1½ cups chicken or vegetable stock,
  or water

3 bulbs baby fennel

juice of ½ lemon

1 tablespoon finely chopped fresh flat-
  leaf parsley

1 tablespoon finely chopped fresh
  cilantro

Moroccan bread, to serve (page 225)

Heat the olive oil in a medium–large tagine or heavy-based saucepan over medium heat. Add the lamb loin chops, red onion, garlic, spices and salt, and cook for 5–10 minutes, stirring occasionally, until the lamb loin chops are browned and the spices are fragrant. Pour in 1¼ cups chicken stock or vegetable stock or water and bring to a boil. Reduce the heat to low, cover and cook for 1¼ hours.

Remove and discard the tough outer layers from the fennel and cut the bulbs into quarters. Arrange the fennel pieces around the lamb loin chops, pour the lemon juice over and sprinkle with the parsley and cilantro. Pour in the remaining chicken or vegetable stock or water, cover and cook for an additional 30–45 minutes, until the meat and fennel are tender.

Serve with Moroccan bread (page 225).

Lamb Tagine with Raisins & Almonds

SERVES 4

2 tablespoons) olive oil

2 tablespoons butter

4 (10½–12-ounce) lamb shanks

2 large red onions, grated

1½ teaspoons ground cinnamon

1½ teaspoons ground ginger

pinch of saffron threads

¼ teaspoon freshly ground black pepper

½ teaspoon salt

1½ cups chicken or vegetable stock, or water

1 cup raisins

¼ cup vegetable oil

½ cup blanched almonds

Moroccan bread, to serve (page 225)

Heat the olive oil and butter in a medium–large tagine or heavy-based saucepan over medium heat. Add the lamb shanks, red onions, spices and salt, and cook for 5–10 minutes, stirring occasionally, until the lamb shanks are browned and the spices are fragrant. Pour in 1¼ cups of the chicken or vegetable stock or water and bring to a boil. Reduce the heat to low, cover and cook for 1½ hours.

Pour in the remaining chicken or vegetable stock or water and scatter with the raisins. Cover and cook for an additional 30 minutes, or until the meat is tender.

Heat the vegetable oil in a small fry pan over low–medium heat. Add the almonds and cook for 2–3 minutes, until golden brown. Scatter the tagine with the almonds and serve with Moroccan bread (page 225).

Lamb Tagine with Tomato & Green Bell Peppers

SERVES 4

2 green bell peppers

¼ cup olive oil

2¾ pounds lamb loin chops

1 large red onion, finely chopped

2 cloves garlic, finely chopped

1 tablespoon paprika

1 teaspoon ground ginger

1 teaspoon ground cumin

¼ teaspoon freshly ground black
  pepper

¼ teaspoon cayenne pepper

pinch of saffron threads

½ teaspoon salt

6 tomatoes, peeled, deseeded and
  chopped

1½ cups chicken or vegetable stock,
  or water

juice of ½ lemon

1 tablespoon finely chopped fresh flat-
  leaf parsley

Moroccan bread, to serve (page 225)

Preheat the oven to 460°F.

Roast the green bell peppers until the skins blister and blacken (about 15 minutes). Place in a bowl, cover with food wrap and set aside to sweat and cool slightly. Peel the green bell peppers and discard the seeds. Slice the flesh into thick lengths and set aside. >

Heat the olive oil in a medium–large tagine or heavy-based saucepan over medium heat. Add the lamb loin chops, red onion, garlic, spices and salt, and cook for 5–10 minutes, stirring occasionally, until the lamb loin chops are browned and the spices are fragrant. Add the tomatoes, then pour in 1¼ cups of the chicken or vegetable stock or water and bring to a boil. Reduce the heat to low, cover and cook for 1½ hours.

Pour in the remaining chicken or vegetable stock or water and the lemon juice. Arrange the bell peppers around the outside of the lamb loin chops and scatter with the parsley. Cover and cook for an additional 30 minutes, or until the meat is tender.

Serve with Moroccan bread (page 225).

Chicken, Prune & Almond Tagine

SERVES 4

2 tablespoons olive oil

1 tablespoon butter

1 (3½ pound) chicken, cut into
  8 pieces

2 large red onions, grated

1½ teaspoons ground cinnamon

1 teaspoon ground ginger

¼ teaspoon freshly ground black
  pepper

pinch of saffron threads

½ teaspoon salt

1¼ cups chicken or vegetable stock,
  or water

1 tablespoon honey

1½ cups pitted prunes

¼ cup vegetable oil

½ cup whole blanched almonds

Moroccan bread, to serve (page 225)

Heat the olive oil and butter in a large tagine or heavy-based saucepan over medium heat. Add the chicken pieces, red onions, spices and salt, and cook for 5–10 minutes, stirring occasionally, until the chicken pieces are browned and the spices are fragrant. Pour in the honey and 1 cup chicken stock or vegetabe stock or water and bring to a boil. Reduce the heat to low, cover and cook for 20 minutes. Scatter with prunes, then pour in the remaining chicken stock or vegetable stock or water, cover and cook for 20–30 minutes, until the chicken pieces are cooked.

Heat the vegetable oil in a small fry pan over low–medium heat. Add the almonds and cook for 2–3 minutes, until golden brown. Sprinkle the almonds over the tagine and serve with Moroccan bread (page 225).

M'qualli Chicken Tagine with Preserved Lemons & Olives

SERVES 4

¼ cup olive oil

1 (3½ pound) chicken, cut into
   8 pieces

1 large red onion, sliced

2 cloves garlic, finely chopped

1½ teaspoons ground ginger

1 teaspoon ground cumin

¼ teaspoon freshly ground black
   pepper

pinch of saffron threads

½ teaspoon salt

1¼ cups chicken or vegetable stock,
   or water

2 preserved lemons, quartered, flesh
   discarded and skin sliced

½ cup green olives

2 tablespoons finely chopped fresh
   flat-leaf parsley

2 tablespoons finely chopped fresh
   cilantro

Moroccan bread, to serve (page 225)

Heat the olive oil in a medium–large tagine or heavy-based saucepan over medium heat. Add the chicken pieces, red onion, garlic, spices and salt, and cook for 5–10 minutes, stirring occasionally, until the chicken pieces are browned and the spices are fragrant. Pour in 1 cup chicken stock or vegetable stock or water and bring to a boil. Reduce the heat to low, cover and cook for 20 minutes.

Arrange the preserved lemons around the chicken pieces and scatter with the green olives. Sprinkle with the parsley and cilantro. Pour in the remaining chicken stock or vegetable stock or water, cover and cook for 25–30 minutes, until the chicken pieces are cooked.

Serve with Moroccan bread (page 225).

Chicken & Apricot Tagine

SERVES 4

¼ cup olive oil

1 (3½ pound) chicken, cut into
8 pieces

1 large red onion, sliced

1 teaspoon ground cinnamon

1 teaspoon ground ginger

¼ teaspoon freshly ground black
pepper

pinch of saffron threads

½ teaspoon salt

1¼ cups chicken or vegetable stock,
or water

1 tablespoon honey

1½ cups dried apricots

2 tablespoons finely chopped fresh
cilantro

Moroccan bread, to serve (page 225)

Heat the olive oil in a medium–large tagine or heavy-based saucepan over medium heat. Add the chicken pieces, red onion, spices and salt, and cook for 5–10 minutes, stirring occasionally, until the chicken pieces are browned and the spices are fragrant. Pour in 1 cup of the chicken stock or vegetable stock or water and the honey, and bring to a boil. Reduce the heat to low, cover and cook for 20 minutes.

Scatter the chicken pieces with dried apricots and cilantro. Pour in the remaining chicken stock or vegetable stock or water, then cover and cook for an additional 25–30 minutes, until the chicken pieces are cooked.

Serve with Moroccan bread (page 225).

Chicken Tagine
with Pumpkin Jam

SERVES 4

1 (3½ pound) chicken, cut into
8 pieces

½ small bunch fresh cilantro, washed
and tied with kitchen string

6 cloves garlic, finely chopped

2 tablespoons olive oil

2 tablespoons butter

1½ teaspoons ground ginger

1 teaspoon ground cumin

¼ teaspoon freshly ground black
pepper

½ teaspoon salt

2 preserved lemons, deseeded and
coarsely chopped

⅓ cup chicken or vegetable stock, or

water

2 medium-sized red onions, quartered

½ cup green olives

PUMPKIN JAM

2 pounds 3 ounces pumpkin, very
finely sliced

1 tablespoon vegetable oil

pinch of salt

3 tablespoons honey

1 tablespoon white granulated sugar

½ teaspoon ground cinnamon

Moroccan bread, to serve (page 225)

To make the pumpkin jam, place the pumpkin slices, vegetable oil and salt in a large non-stick fry pan over low heat. Cover and cook, stirring occasionally, for 20–25 minutes or until the pumpkin slices is soft. Add the honey, granulated white sugar and cinnamon and mash together. Cook, uncovered, for an additional 45–60 minutes, until the pumpkin is thick, sticky and dark orange. Keep warm. >

Place the chicken pieces, cilantro, garlic, olive oil, butter, spices, salt, half of the preserved lemon and half of the chicken stock or vegetable stock or water in a medium–large tagine or heavy-based saucepan over low–medium heat. Reduce the heat to low, cover and cook for 20 minutes. Add the red onions and cook for an additional 25–30 minutes, until the chicken pieces are cooked.

Remove the chicken pieces, set aside on a plate and cover to keep warm. Remove and discard the cilantro.

Mash the onion mixture and liquid together and cook, uncovered, for 10 minutes or until the sauce has thickened. Add the remaining preserved lemons and the green olives and stir to combine.

When the tagine is almost ready to serve, return the chicken pieces to the pot and heat through, coating them in the sauce.

Serve with the pumpkin jam and Moroccan bread (page 225).

Fish & Olive Tagine

SERVES 4

¼ cup olive oil

2 cloves garlic, finely chopped

1 teaspoon ground ginger

½ teaspoon ground turmeric

pinch of saffron threads

¼ teaspoon freshly ground black
  pepper

½ teaspoon salt

4 (7-ounce) snapper fillets, or other
  firm white fish pieces

1 large carrot, sliced into
  ½-inch thick rounds

1 large red onion, sliced into thick
  rounds

2 tomatoes, sliced into thick rounds

1 lemon, sliced into rounds

½ cup green olives

water, to cook fish

2 tablespoons finely chopped fresh
  cilantro

Combine the olive oil, garlic, spices and salt in a large bowl. Add the fish fillets and toss to coat. Cover and place in the refrigerator to marinate for at least 6 hours or overnight.

Arrange the carrot rounds in the bottom of a medium–large tagine or flameproof dish. Cover with half the red onion rounds, followed by the marinated fish fillets and then the remaining red onion rounds. Arrange the tomato and lemon rounds around the fish and scatter with the green olives. Pour in ⅓ cup water and any remaining marinade and sprinkle with the cilantro. Cover and cook over medium heat for 25–30 minutes, until the fish is cooked.

Fish & Saffron Tagine

SERVES 4

2 tablespoons olive oil

2 tablespoons butter

2 large onions, sliced

1 teaspoon ground ginger

¼ teaspoon freshly ground black
    pepper

2 pinches saffron threads

½ teaspoon salt

1 large carrot, cut into ½-inch thick
    rounds

2¾ pounds snapper, or other firm
    white fish, cut into 4-inch pieces

1 preserved lemon, quartered, flesh
    discarded and skin sliced

water, to cook fish

Moroccan bread, to serve (page 225)

Heat the olive oil and butter in a medium-sized fry pan over low–medium heat.

Add the onions, spices and salt, and sauté until softened and fragrant.

Arrange the carrot rounds in the bottom of a medium–large tagine or flameproof dish. Layer half of the spiced onion mixture on top, followed by the pieces of fish and then the remaining onions. Arrange the preserved lemon quarters around the fish. Pour in ⅓ cup water. Cover and cook over medium heat for 25–30 minutes, until the pieces of fish are cooked.

Serve with Moroccan bread (page 225).

Fish-ball Tagine

SERVES 4

2 pounds 3 ounces grouper fillets, or other firm white fish fillets, skin and bones removed

2 tablespoons fine soft breadcrumbs

1 small carrot, cut into rounds

1 tablespoon finely chopped fresh cilantro

CHERMOULA PASTE

2 cloves garlic, chopped

2 tablespoons finely chopped fresh cilantro leaves

2 tablespoons finely chopped fresh flat-leaf parsley leaves

1 tablespoon olive oil

1 tablespoon lemon juice

1 teaspoon paprika

1 teaspoon ground cumin

1 teaspoon ground coriander

¼ teaspoon freshly ground black pepper

½ teaspoon salt

TOMATO SAUCE

2 tablespoons olive oil

1 onion, finely chopped

2 teaspoons granulated white sugar

1 teaspoon ground cumin

1 teaspoon paprika

½ teaspoon ground turmeric

8 tomatoes, peeled, deseeded and coarsely chopped

water, to prepare tomato sauce

salt and freshly ground black pepper

Moroccan bread, to serve (page 225)

To make the chermoula paste, place the garlic, cilantro and parsley in a food processor or blender and blend to a paste. Add the olive oil, lemon juice, spices and salt and blend to combine. ❯

Coarsely chop the fish fillets and pass through a grater or mincer, or finely chop in a food processor or blender. Combine the minced fish, chermoula paste and breadcrumbs in a medium-sized bowl. Shape into walnut-sized balls, cover and refrigerate until needed.

To make the tomato sauce, heat the olive oil in a large fry pan over low–medium heat. Add the onion, sugar and spices, and sauté until softened and fragrant. Add the tomatoes and cook for 5 minutes, until softened. Pour in ⅓ cup water and bring to a boil. Season with salt and freshly ground black pepper.

Spoon half of the tomato sauce into the bottom of a medium–large tagine or flameproof dish and arrange the fish balls on top. Cover with the remaining sauce and sprinkle with the cilantro. Cover and cook over low–medium heat for 15–20 minutes, until the fish is cooked.

Serve with Moroccan bread (page 225).

Fish, Date & Onion Tagine

SERVES 4

2 tablespoons olive oil

2 tablespoons butter

1 tablespoon honey

2 large red onions, cut into rounds

1 teaspoon ground ginger

1 teaspoon ground cinnamon

¼ teaspoon freshly ground black
   pepper

pinch of saffron threads

½ teaspoon salt

1½ cups pitted dried dates

1 large carrot, cut into ½-inch thick
   rounds

4 (7-ounce) snapper fillets, or other
   firm white fish

water, to cook fish

¼ cup vegetable oil

¼ cup whole blanched almonds

Moroccan bread, to serve (page 225)

Heat the olive oil, butter and honey in a fry pan over low–medium heat. Add the red onions, spices and salt, and sauté until softened. Stir in the dates.

Arrange the carrot rounds in the bottom of a medium–large tagine. Layer half the onion mixture on top, followed by the fish fillets and the remaining onion mixture. Pour in ⅓ cup water, cover and cook over medium heat for 25–30 minutes.

Heat the vegetable oil in a small fry pan over low–medium heat. Add the almonds and cook for 2–3 minutes, until golden brown. Scatter the tagine with almonds and serve with Moroccan bread.

Fish, Tomato & Zucchini Tagine

SERVES 4

2 tablespoons olive oil

1 large red onion, finely chopped

1 teaspoon ground coriander

1 teaspoon ground cumin

½ teaspoon ground turmeric

¼ teaspoon freshly ground black pepper

pinch of saffron threads

½ teaspoon salt

4 tomatoes, peeled, deseeded and coarsely chopped

water, to prepare tomato sauce

1 preserved lemon, flesh discarded and skin coarsely chopped

1 large carrot, cut into ½-inch thick rounds

4 (6½-ounce) thick swordfish steaks

2 medium-sized zucchini, quartered lengthwise and deseeded

2 tablespoons finely chopped fresh cilantro

Moroccan bread, to serve (page 225)

Heat the olive oil in a medium-sized fry pan over low–medium heat. Add the red onion, spices and salt, and sauté until softened and fragrant.

Add the tomatoes to the pan and cook for 5 minutes, until softened. Pour in ⅓ cup water and bring to a boil. Decrease the heat to low, add the preserved lemon and stir to combine.

Arrange the carrot rounds in the bottom of a medium–large tagine or flameproof dish. Spoon half of the sauce over the carrots and lay the sword fish steaks on top. Arrange the zucchini around the sword fish steaks and cover the fish and zucchini with the remaining sauce. Sprinkle with the cilantro, cover and cook over medium heat for 25–30 minutes, until the fish is cooked.

Serve with Moroccan bread (page 225).

Spicy Tuna, Potato & Green Bell Pepper Tagine

SERVES 4

4 (6½-ounce) thick tuna steaks

1 large carrot, sliced into ³/₈-inch
thick rounds

1 large red onion, sliced into rounds

2 medium-sized potatoes, thickly
sliced lengthwise

2 green bell peppers, sliced into
³/₈-inch thick rings

1 lemon, sliced into rounds

water, to cook tuna steaks

Moroccan bread, to serve (page 225)

CHERMOULA PASTE

3 cloves garlic, chopped

½ bunch fresh coriander, leaves
chopped

½ bunch fresh flat-leaf parsley, leaves
chopped

¼ cup olive oil

¼ cup lemon juice

1½ teaspoons paprika

1 teaspoon ground cumin

1 teaspoon ground coriander

½ teaspoon freshly ground black
pepper

½ teaspoon salt

To make the chermoula paste, place the garlic, cilantro and parsley in a food processor or blender and blend to a paste. Add the olive oil, lemon juice, spices and salt, and blend to combine.

Combine the tuna steaks and chermoula paste in a large bowl and toss to coat. Cover and place in the refrigerator to marinate for at least 6 hours or overnight. ❯

Arrange the carrot rounds in the bottom of a medium–large tagine or flameproof dish. Layer the red onion rounds on top, followed by the marinated tuna steaks. Arrange the potato slices and green bell pepper rings around the tuna steaks. Top with the lemon rounds and pour in ⅓ cup water and any remaining marinade. Cover and cook over medium heat for 25–30 minutes, until the tuna steaks are cooked.

Serve with Moroccan bread (page 225).

Vegetable Tagine

SERVES 4

¼ cup olive oil

1 large red onion, sliced

2 cloves garlic, finely chopped

1 teaspoon paprika

1 teaspoon ground ginger

1 teaspoon ground cumin

½ teaspoon ground turmeric

½ teaspoon cayenne pepper

¼ teaspoon freshly ground black
  pepper

pinch of saffron threads

½ teaspoon salt

2 medium-sized carrots, quartered
  lengthwise and cored

1 sweet potato, sliced into rounds

2 medium-sized potatoes, thickly
  sliced lengthwise

2 medium-sized zucchini, quartered
  lengthwise and deseeded

2 tomatoes, peeled, deseeded and
  coarsely chopped

1 green bell pepper, thickly sliced
  lengthwise

½ cup fresh or frozen peas

2 tablespoons finely chopped fresh
  flat-leaf parsley

2 tablespoons finely chopped fresh
  cilantro

1/3 cup vegetable stock or water

Moroccan bread, to serve (page 225)

Heat the olive oil in a medium–large tagine or heavy-based saucepan over medium heat. Add the red onion, garlic, spices and salt, and sauté until softened and fragrant. **>**

Arrange the vegetables in the tagine in layers, starting with the carrots, then the sweet potato rounds, potatoes, zucchini, tomatoes and green bell pepper. Scatter with the peas and sprinkle with the parsley and cilantro.

Pour in the vegetable stock or water and bring to a boil. Reduce the heat to low, cover and cook for 20–30 minutes, or until the vegetables are tender.

Serve with Moroccan bread (page 225).

Pumpkin & Sweet Potato Tagine

SERVES 4

¼ cup olive oil

2 medium-sized red onions, sliced

3 cloves garlic, finely chopped

1 teaspoon ground ginger

1 teaspoon ground cinnamon

½ teaspoon ground turmeric

½ teaspoon cayenne pepper

¼ teaspoon freshly ground black pepper

pinch of saffron threads

½ teaspoon salt

1 pound pumpkin, cut into 1½-inch cubes

1 pound sweet potatoes, cut into 1½-inch cubes

¾ cup vegetable stock or water

¼ cup vegetable oil

½ cup whole blanched almonds

Heat the olive oil in a medium–large tagine or heavy-based saucepan over medium heat. Add the red onions, garlic, spices and salt, and sauté until softened and fragrant. Add the pumpkin and sweet potato cubes and cook, stirring, for 5–10 minutes or until golden brown. Pour in the vegetable stock or water and bring to a boil. Decrease the heat to low, cover and cook for 20–30 minutes, until the pumpkin and sweet potato cubes are tender.

Heat the vegetable oil in a small fry pan over low–medium heat. Add the almonds and cook for 2–3 minutes, until golden brown. Drain on paper towels. Sprinkle the almonds over the tagine and serve.

Zucchini, Tomato & Chickpea Tagine

SERVES 4

1 cup dried chickpeas (garbanzo, or ceci beans)

cold water, to soak and cook chickpeas

¼ cup olive oil

1 large red onion, sliced

2 cloves garlic, finely chopped

1 teaspoon paprika

1 teaspoon ground cumin

½ teaspoon ground ginger

½ teaspoon ground turmeric

½ teaspoon cayenne pepper

¼ teaspoon freshly ground black pepper

½ teaspoon salt

4 medium-sized tomatoes, peeled and quartered

2 medium-sized zucchini, quartered and deseeded

2 tablespoons finely chopped fresh flat-leaf parsley

2 tablespoons finely chopped fresh cilantro

¹/₃ cup vegetable stock or water

Soak the chickpeas in cold water for at least 6 hours or overnight. Drain and rinse the chickpeas and place in a medium-sized saucepan. Cover with cold water and bring to a boil over high heat. Cook for 1 hour, until tender. Drain and set aside.

Heat the olive oil in a medium–large tagine or heavy-based saucepan over medium heat. Add the red onion, garlic, spices and salt, and sauté until softened and fragrant. Add the chickpeas, tomatoes, zucchini, parsley and cilantro and stir to combine. Pour in the vegetable stock or water and bring to a boil. Reduce the heat to low, cover and cook for 20–30 minutes, until the vegetables are tender.

Spicy Pumpkin & Lentil Tagine

SERVES 4–6

½ cup dried green lentils

1 quart 2 ounces vegetable stock or
water

¼ cup olive oil

1 large brown skinned onion, sliced

3 cloves garlic, finely chopped

2 teaspoons paprika

1 teaspoon ground turmeric

1 teaspoon ground cumin

½ teaspoon cayenne pepper

¼ teaspoon freshly ground black
pepper

½ teaspoon salt

2 tomatoes, peeled, deseeded and
coarsely chopped

3 teaspoons tomato paste

1 pound 9 ounces pumpkin, cut into
1½–inch cubes

¼ cup raisins

2 tablespoons chopped fresh flat-leaf
parsley

2 tablespoons chopped fresh cilantro

Place the lentils and vegetable stock or water in a medium-sized saucepan over medium–high heat and bring to a boil. Decrease the heat to low, cover and cook for 15–20 minutes, until the lentils are just tender. Set aside.

Heat the olive oil in a medium–large tagine or heavy-based saucepan over medium heat. Add the onion, garlic, spices and salt, and sauté until softened and fragrant. Add the tomatoes and tomato paste, and stir to combine. Add the pumpkin cubes and undrained lentils. Scatter with the raisins and bring to a boil. Decrease the heat to low, cover and cook for 20–30 minutes, until the pumpkin is tender. Sprinkle with the parsley and cilantro.

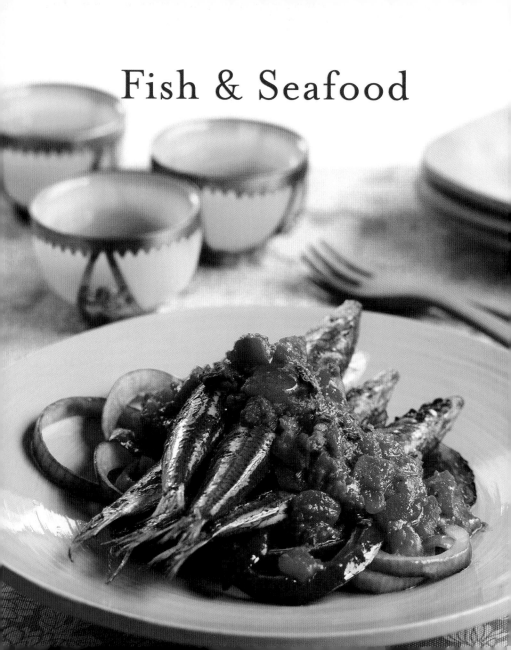

Fish & Seafood

Fish and seafood are found in abundance in the Moroccan towns and villages that line the Atlantic coast. Fish and seafood fresh off the boat are sold at markets daily.

You can even take fish and seafood from the market straight to a nearby food stall where they will be cooked over hot coals, then seasoned simply with sea salt and a drizzle of oil.

< Grilled Sardines (page 122)

Grilled Sardines

SERVES 4

2 large red onions, sliced into rounds

4 pounds 6 ounces whole fresh
   sardines, scaled and gutted

drizzle of olive oil

salt and freshly ground black pepper

2 lemons, cut into wedges

HARISSA-SPICED TOMATO
SAUCE

1 tablespoon olive oil

4 medium-sized tomatoes, peeled,
   deseeded and finely chopped

2 tablespoons harissa paste (page 233)

1 tablespoon lemon juice

½ cup finely chopped fresh cilantro

salt and freshly ground black pepper

To make the harissa-spiced tomato sauce, heat the olive oil in a large fry pan over low–medium heat. Add the tomatoes and sauté for 5 minutes, until softened. Add the harissa paste, lemon juice and cilantro, stir to combine, and cook for an additional 2 minutes. Season with salt and freshly ground black pepper. Cover and refrigerate until required.

Preheat barbecue to medium–high.

Spread one-quarter of the red onion rounds on a flat wire grill pan that can be closed and secured. Lay half of the sardines on top of the onion rounds and cover with another one-quarter of the red onion rounds. Close and secure the grill pan. Drizzle with olive oil and sprinkle with salt and freshly ground black pepper on both sides of the sardines. Cook the sardines for 5 minutes on each side, until cooked through.

Repeat the process with the remaining sardines and red onion rounds.

Serve with the lemon wedges and harissa-spiced tomato sauce.

Trout Filled with Stuffed Dates

SERVES 4

2 (2 pound 3-ounce) whole trout,
scaled and cleaned

drizzle of olive oil

salt and freshly ground black pepper

¼ cup sliced almonds

STUFFED DATES

water, to cook rice

¼ cup long-grain rice, rinsed

7 tablespoons butter

1 medium-sized red onion, finely
chopped

1 teaspoon ground cinnamon

1 teaspoon ground ginger

¾ cup ground almonds

1 pound fresh dates, pitted

Preheat the oven to 360°F.

To make the stuffed dates, bring a small saucepan of water to a boil. Add the rice and cook for 3 minutes. Drain and set aside to cool.

Melt 2 tablespoons of the butter in a small fry pan over low–medium heat. Add the red onion and spices, and sauté until the onion is soft and the spices are fragrant.

Combine the cooled rice, spiced red onion and ground almonds in a medium-sized bowl, mixing well. Stuff the dates with the rice filling and place inside the trout cavities, along with any remaining filling. Secure the edges of the cavities using toothpicks.

Lay each whole trout on a sheet of aluminum foil large enough to enclose it. Drizzle with olive oil and season with salt and freshly ground black pepper. Dot with the remaining butter and sprinkle with the sliced almonds. Wrap the aluminum foil around each fish to enclose completely.

Bake in the oven for 15–25 minutes, until cooked through and the flesh flakes easily. Remove the toothpicks and serve.

Grilled Chermoula Fish

SERVES 4

1 (3 pound 5-ounce) whole snapper, scaled and cleaned

3 medium-sized tomatoes, sliced into rounds

1 large red onion, sliced into rounds

2 lemons, cut into wedges

CHERMOULA PASTE

3 cloves garlic, chopped

½ bunch fresh cilantro, leaves chopped

½ bunch fresh flat-leaf parsley, leaves chopped

¼ cup olive oil

¼ cup lemon juice

1½ teaspoons paprika

1 teaspoon ground cumin

1 teaspoon ground coriander

½ teaspoon freshly ground black pepper

½ teaspoon salt

To make the chermoula paste, place the garlic, cilantro and parsley in a food processor or blender and blend to a paste. Add the olive oil, lemon juice, spices and salt and blend to combine.

Score the whole snapper twice in the thickest part near the head to ensure even cooking. Place the whole snapper in a large dish and coat with chermoula, filling the cavity and scored cuts. Cover and place in the refrigerator to marinate for at least 6 hours or overnight.

Preheat the oven to 390°F. **>**

Lay half the tomato and onion rounds in the bottom of a large baking dish. Place the marinated whole snapper on top and cover with the remaining tomato and onion rounds. Bake in the oven for 25–30 minutes, until cooked through and the flesh flakes easily.

Serve with lemon wedges.

Fish with Preserved Lemons & Olives

SERVES 4

1 (3 pound 5-ounce) whole snapper, grouper, orange roughy or mahi mahi, scaled and cleaned

¼ cup olive oil

¼ cup lemon juice

1 clove garlic, crushed

1½ teaspoons ground ginger

1 teaspoon ground cumin

½ teaspoon ground turmeric

¼ teaspoon freshly ground black pepper

½ teaspoon salt

2 preserved lemons, quartered, flesh discarded and skin finely sliced

1 small red onion, sliced

¼ cup green olives

Score the fish twice in the thickest part near the head to make sure that it cooks evenly, and place in a large dish.

Combine the olive oil, lemon juice, garlic, spices and salt in a medium-sized bowl. Add the preserved lemons and red onion slices. Pour the mixture over the whole fish, rubbing to coat and filling the cavity and scored cuts. Cover and place in the refrigerator to marinate for at least 6 hours or overnight.

Preheat the oven to 390°F.

Lay the marinated whole fish on a sheet of aluminum foil large enough to enclose it. Scatter with the green olives, drizzle with any remaining marinade and wrap the aluminum foil around the whole fish, folding the edges to seal. Bake for 25–30 minutes, until cooked through and the flesh flakes easily.

Fried Fish with Chermoula Paste

SERVES 4

1 cup semolina (coarse grain) flour

1 teaspoon ground cumin

1 teaspoon ground ginger

½ teaspoon freshly ground black
  pepper

1 teaspoon salt

2 large eggs

2 pounds catfish tails

vegetable oil, for deep-frying

2 lemons, cut into wedges

CHERMOULA PASTE

3 cloves garlic, chopped

½ bunch fresh cilantro, leaves
  chopped

½ bunch fresh flat-leaf parsley, leaves
  chopped

¼ cup olive oil

¼ cup lemon juice

1½ teaspoons paprika

1 teaspoon ground cumin

1 teaspoon ground coriander

½ teaspoon freshly ground black
  pepper

½ teaspoon salt

To make the chermoula paste, place the garlic, cilantro and parsley in a food processor or blender and blend to a paste. Add the olive oil, lemon juice, spices and salt and blend to combine.

To prepare the catfish tails, combine the semolina flour, spices and salt in a medium-sized bowl. Lightly beat the eggs in a separate bowl. Coat the catfish tails by dipping each one in the beaten eggs followed by the spiced semolina flour.

Preheat the vegetable oil in a large, heavy-based fry pan suitable for deep-frying. Fry the catfish tails in batches for 1–2 minutes on each side, or until cooked through. Drain on paper towels and keep warm until all the catfish tails are cooked.

Serve with lemon wedges and chermoula paste for dipping.

Harissa Prawns

SERVES 4

2¾ pounds raw (green) tiger prawns, shelled and deveined

salt and freshly ground black pepper

2 lemons, cut into wedges

HARISSA MARINADE

¼ cup olive oil

2 tablespoons lemon juice

2 tablespoons ground almonds

1 tablespoon finely chopped fresh flat-leaf parsley

1 tablespoon finely chopped fresh cilantro

1 clove garlic, crushed

2 teaspoons harissa paste (page 233)

1 teaspoon paprika

½ teaspoon ground cumin

½ teaspoon ground ginger

½ teaspoon ground turmeric

Combine all the marinade ingredients in a medium-sized bowl. Add the tiger prawns and toss to coat. Season with salt and freshly ground black pepper. Cover and place in the refrigerator to marinate for at least 6 hours or overnight.

Preheat a large non-stick fry pan over high heat. Cook the tiger prawns with the marinade for 1–2 minutes on each side, or until they turn pink and begin to firm.

Serve with the lemon wedges.

❊ Tiger prawns are large shrimp. Medium-sized shrimp may be substituted.

Stewed Octopus

SERVES 4

1 (2¾-pound) octopus

cold water, to cook octopus

2 tablespoons olive oil

1 large red onion, finely chopped

1 clove garlic, finely chopped

1 bay leaf

1 teaspoon paprika

½ teaspoon ground cumin

¼ teaspoon cayenne pepper

4 medium-sized tomatoes, peeled, deseeded and coarsely chopped

juice of 1 lemon

½ cup finely chopped fresh cilantro

salt and freshly ground black pepper

steamed or boiled long-grain rice, to serve

Wash the octopus under cold running water and remove the organs and the ink sac. Place the octopus in a large saucepan, cover with cold water and bring to a boil. Decrease the heat to medium and simmer for 1 hour. Drain and set the octopus aside to cool slightly.

Peel the thin outer membrane off the octopus. Remove and discard the head, cutting away the beak. Cut the remaining flesh and tentacles into ¾-inch thick pieces.

Heat the olive oil in a medium-sized saucepan over low–medium heat. Add the red onion, garlic, bay leaf and spices, and sauté until softened and fragrant. Add the octopus, tomatoes and lemon juice, and cook over low heat for 20–25 minutes, until the sauce is thick and the octopus tender. Add the cilantro and season with salt and freshly ground black pepper.

To serve, pile the rice onto a large serving plate and spoon the octopus and sauce over the top.

Seafood Bastilla

SERVES 6–8

7 ounces vermicelli rice noodles

water, to cook noodles

1 cup fish stock

juice of 1 lemon

2 pounds 3 ounces cod, haddock, hake
or pollock fillets

¼ cup olive oil

1 large red onion, finely chopped

1 teaspoon ground ginger

1 teaspoon ground turmeric

1 teaspoon ground cumin

½ teaspoon cayenne pepper

pinch of saffron threads, crushed

1 pound 2 ounces raw (green) prawns,
shelled, deveined and cut in half

1 pound 2 ounces squid tubes, cleaned
and cut into ⁵⁄₈-inch thick rings

3 tablespoons finely chopped fresh
flat-leaf parsley

3 tablespoons finely chopped fresh
cilantro

1 preserved lemon, quartered, flesh
discarded and skin finely chopped

salt and freshly ground black pepper

10 sheets filo pastry

10 tablepoons butter, melted

1 cup grated cheese (Edam, Gouda,
mild Cheddar or Swiss)

1 large egg yolk, lightly beaten

Preheat the oven to 390°F. Grease a deep 12-inch pizza pan.

Soak the vermicelli noodles in boiling water for 5 minutes, until softened. Drain,
chop coarsely and set aside.

Pour the fish stock and lemon juice into a large saucepan and bring to a boil.

Reduce the heat to low, add the fish fillets and poach gently for 3–4 minutes on each side, until cooked through. Remove the fish fillets, reserving the liquid, and flake into large chunks. Place in a large bowl and set aside.

Sauté the red onion and spices in a large saucepan until softened. Increase the heat to high, add the prawns and cook for 1 minute. Add the squid tubes and cook for 2–3 minutes, until the prawns turn pink and the squid tubes turn white. Remove the seafood from the pan and add to the chunks of fish. Pour the reserved stock into the pan and simmer until reduced to about 2 tablespoons. Add the reduced stock, vermicelli noodles, herbs and preserved lemon to the seafood. Stir to combine and season with salt and freshly ground black pepper.

Brush one sheet of filo pastry with melted butter, fold in half and place in the bottom of the pizza pan. Repeat with another eight sheets of filo pastry. Arrange the sheets, overlapping, to cover the sides of the pan, leaving one-third of the filo pastry hanging over the edge.

Pour the fish and seafood mixture into the filo pastry-lined pan and sprinkle with the cheese. Fold the filo pastry over the filling to enclose, brushing in between layers with melted butter to seal. Brush around the edge with the egg yolk and lay the last sheet of filo pastry over the top. Carefully tuck the edges under the top to form a round pie. Brush the top with melted butter and egg yolk. Pierce a few holes in the top with a skewer. Bake in the oven for 15–20 minutes, until crisp and golden-brown.

Veal, Lamb
& Chicken

Chicken, Morocco's most popular poultry, is usually steamed or roasted, and stuffed with various fillings such as couscous, rice, vermicelli noodles, kefta or almonds. Try making Morocco's famous chicken bastilla (page 152). This rich pie is layered with eggs, chicken and sweet roasted almonds, wrapped in crisp warka pastry and dusted with sugar and cinnamon. It takes some time to make, but it is definitely worth the effort.

In Moroccan cuisine, meat is always slow-cooked, gently spiced and heavily basted. The end result is tender, fall-off-the-bone morsels, which are eaten with the fingers or wrapped in freshly baked bread.

❋ Kefta is ground meat, particularly beef or lamb, or in combination.

❋ Warka pastry is paper-thin pastry, similar to filo pastry.

< Slow-cooked Veal Stew (page 140)

Slow-cooked Veal Stew

Tangia

SERVES 6

3 pounds 5 ounces veal osso bucco

2 large red onions, grated

2 preserved lemons, quartered and
deseeded

4 cloves garlic, finely chopped

1½ tablespoons ground cumin

¼ teaspoon freshly ground black
pepper

¼ teaspoon ground turmeric

pinch of saffron threads, crumbled

½ teaspoon salt

8 tablespoons butter, cubed

water, to cook veal osso bucco

Preheat the oven to 250°F.

Place the veal osso bucco, red onions, preserved lemons, garlic, spices and salt in a large baking dish and toss to coat. Dot with the butter and pour in 2 cups water. Cover with a piece of parchment (baking) paper, followed by aluminum foil, and secure tightly. Cook in the oven for 8 hours, until the meat is tender and falling off the bone.

Spicy Lamb

SERVES 8

1 (5 pound 5-ounce) leg of lamb

10 tablespoons butter, softened

2 cloves garlic, crushed

2 teaspoons ground cumin

½ teaspoon freshly ground black
   pepper

½ teaspoon cayenne pepper

1 teaspoon salt

2 large red onions, quartered

½ bunch fresh flat-leaf parsley

½ bunch fresh lemon thyme

3 bay leaves

2 tablespoons olive oil

Trim the leg of lamb of fat and make ⅝-inch deep incisions into the flesh. Combine half of the butter with all of the garlic, spices and salt in a small bowl. Rub over the leg of lamb and into the incisions, then wrap in a large piece of cheese cloth.

Fill the bottom of a large steamer saucepan one-third full with with water, place over high heat and bring to a boil. Arrange the red onions and herbs in the top steamer section of the saucepan. Put the wrapped lamb leg on top, making sure that it is sealed completely. (Wrap aluminum foil around the rim of the saucepan if necessary to seal.) Cover and steam the leg of lamb for 2–2½ hours or until the meat is tender and almost falling off the bone. Remove the leg of lamb from the steamer.

Melt the remaining butter in a large flameproof baking dish over high heat and brown the leg of lamb on all sides. Transfer to a serving dish.

M'hammer-spiced Lamb

SERVES 6

3 pounds 5 ounces shoulder of lamb

10 tablespoons butter, softened

2 cloves garlic, crushed

2 teaspoons paprika

1 teaspoon ground cumin

1 teaspoon cayenne pepper

½ teaspoon freshly ground black
   pepper

½ teaspoon ground turmeric

pinch of saffron threads, crumbled

1 teaspoon salt

2 large red onions, finely chopped

½ cup finely chopped fresh cilantro

water, to cook shoulder of lamb

Trim the shoulder of lamb of fat and make ⅝-inch deep incisions into the flesh. Combine half of the butter with all of the garlic, spices and salt in a bowl. Rub over the shoulder of lamb and into the incisions.

Put half of the red onions in a large, heavy-based saucepan and sprinkle with half of the cilantro. Place the shoulder of lamb on top and sprinkle with the remaining red onions and cilantro. Pour in 1½ cups water and bring to a boil. Decrease the heat to low–medium and cook, basting occasionally, for 1½–2 hours, until the meat is tender and almost falling off the bone.

Melt the remaining butter in a large flameproof baking dish over high heat and brown the shoulder of lamb, turning on all sides. Transfer to a serving dish and cover with aluminum foil to keep warm.

Add the butter to the remaining liquid in the saucepan. Place over medium–high heat and simmer until thickened into a sauce. Pour over the shoulder of lamb.

❋ M'hammer is a red sauce that is based on butter, paprika and cumin.

Spiced Lamb Stuffed with Kefta

SERVES 8

1 (4 pound 6-ounce) leg of lamb,
  boned

2 tablespoons olive oil

1 teaspoon paprika

½ teaspoon ground cumin

salt and freshly ground black pepper

1 large red onion, coarsely chopped

water, to cook leg of lamb

KEFTA STUFFING

¼ cup olive oil

1 small red onion, grated

2 cloves garlic, crushed

½ teaspoon ground cumin

½ teaspoon ground cinnamon

¼ teaspoon ground ginger

¼ teaspoon paprika

pinch of freshly ground black pepper

pinch of cayenne pepper

¼ teaspoon salt

4½ ounces coarsley ground lamb

3½ ounces chicken livers, finely
  chopped

2 tablespoons finely chopped fresh
  flat-leaf parsley

2 tablespoons finely chopped fresh
  cilantro

1 large egg

Trim the leg of lamb of any excess fat. Make a cut into the flesh, but not all the way through, and butterfly the meat, opening it out so that it can wrap and enclose the filling.

To make the kefta stuffing, heat the olive oil in a medium-sized fry pan over low–medium heat. Add the red onion, garlic, spices and salt and sauté until softened and fragrant. Remove from the heat and transfer to a medium-sized bowl. Add the coarsely ground lamb, chicken livers, parsley, cilantro and egg and mix well to combine.

Spread the stuffing over the inside of the butterflied leg of lamb. Wrap the meat around to enclose the kefta stuffing and tie up with kitchen string.

Combine the olive oil, paprika and cumin and rub over the leg of lamb. Season with salt and freshly ground black pepper. Put the red onion in the bottom of a large saucepan and place the leg of lamb on top. Pour in 1 cup water and bring to a boil. Decrease the heat to low, cover and cook for 1½–2 hours, until tender.

Preheat the oven to 390°F.

Take the leg of lamb out of the saucepan and transfer to a large baking dish. Bake in the oven for 15–20 minutes, until browned.

Slow-roasted Leg of Lamb

Mechoui

SERVES 8

1 (5 pound 5-ounce) leg of lamb

8 tablespoons butter, softened

3 cloves garlic, crushed

1 tablespoon paprika

2 teaspoons ground cumin

2 teaspoons ground coriander

½ teaspoon freshly ground black pepper

½ teaspoon cayenne pepper

½ teaspoon ground cinnamon

1 teaspoon salt

Preheat the oven to 420°F.

Trim the leg of lamb of any excess fat and make ⅝-inch deep incisions into the flesh.

Combine the butter, garlic, spices and salt in a bowl. Rub over the leg of lamb and into the incisions. Place the leg of lamb in a large baking dish and pour in 1 cup water. Bake in the oven on the top rack for 20 minutes.

Move the leg of lamb to the middle rack, reduce the heat to 320°F and bake for an additional 3 hours, until the meat is tender and almost falling off the bone. Baste with the pan juices every 15 minutes to keep the leg of lamb moist and flavorsome.

Lamb with Hard-boiled Eggs & Almonds

Tafaya

SERVES 6

2 pounds 3 ounces boneless lamb shoulder or leg

¼ ounces olive oil

1 large red onion, grated

2 cloves garlic, finely chopped

1½ teaspoons ground ginger

½ teaspoon ground cinnamon

¼ teaspoon freshly ground black pepper

pinch of saffron threads, crumbled

½ teaspoon salt

water, to cook lamb

½ cup finely chopped fresh cilantro

2 tablespoons vegetable oil

1 cup blanched almonds

6 hard-boiled eggs, peeled and halved lengthwise

Trim the lamb of tough connective tissue and excess fat and cut into large cubes of approximately 2 inches.

Heat the olive oil in a large, heavy-based saucepan or flameproof dish over medium heat. Add the lamb, red onion, garlic, spices and salt and cook for 5–10 minutes, stirring occasionally, until the lamb is browned and the spices are fragrant. Pour in 2 cups water and bring to a boil. Reduce the heat to low, cover and cook for 1½ hours. ❯

Add the cilantro and stir to combine. Cook for an additional 30 minutes, until the meat is tender.

Heat the vegetable oil in a medium-sized fry pan over low–medium heat. Add the almonds and cook until golden brown. Remove using a slotted spoon and drain on paper towels.

Arrange the lamb on a serving plate and cover with sauce. Decorate with the egg halves and scatter with the almonds.

Lamb Stuffed with Couscous

SERVES 8

1 (4 pound 6-ounce) leg of lamb, boned

6 tablespoons butter, softened

2 cloves garlic, crushed

1 teaspoon paprika

½ teaspoon ground cumin

¼ teaspoon freshly ground black pepper

¼ teaspoon cayenne pepper

½ teaspoon salt

water, to cook lamb

COUSCOUS STUFFING

¾ cup couscous

1¼ cups water with 1 teaspoon salt

1 tablespoon olive oil

¼ cup raisins

boiling water, to cover raisins

1 tablespoon vegetable oil

¼ cup slivered almonds

1 tablespoon butter

½ teaspoon ground cinnamon

½ teaspoon ground cumin

¼ teaspoon ground ginger

2 tablespoons finely chopped fresh flat-leaf parsley

salt and freshly ground black pepper

To make the couscous stuffing, follow the method for traditional Moroccan couscous on page 54, using ½ cup salted water in the first step. Add the remaining salted water and the olive oil during step two, or follow the package instructions for instant couscous.

Place the raisins in a small bowl and cover with boiling water. Set aside for 10 minutes to plump. Drain.

Heat the vegetable oil in a medium-sized fry pan over low–medium heat. Add the slivered almonds and cook until golden brown. Remove using a slotted spoon and drain on paper towels.

Add the butter, raisins, slivered almonds, spices and parsley to the couscous and mix in using your fingers. Season with salt and freshly ground black pepper.

Preheat the oven to 420°F.

Spread the prepared couscous over the butterflied leg of lamb. Wrap the meat around to enclose and tie with kitchen string.

Place any excess couscous in a small baking pan and cover with aluminum foil, ready to heat in the oven 20 minutes before the leg of lamb is ready to serve.

Combine the butter, garlic, spices and salt and rub over the leg of lamb. Place the leg of lamb in a large baking dish and pour in 1 cup water. Bake in the oven on the top rack for 20 minutes. Move the lamb to the middle rack, reduce the heat to 360°F and bake for an additional 2–2½ hours or until the meat is tender and almost falling off the bone. Baste with the pan juices occasionally to keep the leg of lamb moist and flavorsome.

Chicken Bastilla

SERVES 8–10

1 (3 pound 5-ounce) chicken, wings
   discarded

3 medium-sized brown-skinned
   onions, roughly chopped

2 teaspoons ground ginger

1 teaspoon ground turmeric

pinch of saffron threads

salt and freshly ground black pepper

¾ cup vegetable oil

1 tablespoon butter

water, to cook chicken

3 cups roughly chopped fresh flat-leaf
   parsley

3 tablespoons roughly chopped fresh
   cilantro

2 tablespoons granulated white sugar

1 teaspoon ground cinnamon, plus
   extra to garnish

10 large eggs, lightly beaten, plus
   1 large egg yolk

10 sheets filo pastry

7 tablespoons butter, melted

confectioner's (powdered) sugar, to
   garnish

ALMOND FILLING

¹/₃ cup vegetable oil

3 cups blanched almonds

2 tablespoons granulated white sugar

Place the chicken, onions, spices, salt, vegetable oil and butter in a large sauce-pan and turn to coat. Cover and cook over low–medium heat for 30 minutes. Pour in 1½ cups water, cover and cook for 30–45 minutes.

To make the almond filling, heat the vegetable oil in a fry pan over low–medium heat. Add almonds and cook until golden. Drain on paper towels and allow to cool. ❯

Blend the almonds and granulated white sugar in a food processor or blender to make fine crumbs.

Remove the chicken from the saucepan, reserving the liquid, and set aside to cool slightly. Strip the meat off the bones, roughly shred and set aside.

Heat the reserved cooking liquid over low–medium heat. Add the herbs, sugar and cinnamon and stir to combine. Gradually pour in the beaten eggs, stirring constantly until thickened. Take off the heat and set aside.

Preheat the oven to 390°F. Grease a deep 12-inch pizza pan. Brush one sheet of filo pastry with melted butter, fold in half and place in the bottom of the pizza pan. Repeat with another eight sheets of filo pastry. Arrange the sheets, overlapping, to cover the sides of the pan, leaving one-third of the filo pastry hanging over the edge of the pan.

Pour the egg mixture into the pastry-filled pan. Create a second layer with the chicken and a final layer with the almond mixture. Wrap the overhanging pastry over the filling to enclose, brushing in between layers with butter to seal. Brush around the edge with egg yolk and lay the final sheet of filo pastry over the top. Carefully tuck the edges under the top to form a round pie. Brush the top with butter and egg yolk. Pierce a few holes in the top to allow the steam to escape. Bake in the oven for 15–20 minutes, until crisp and golden brown.

To decorate, dust the top of the pie with confectioner's (powdered) sugar and create a lattice pattern with thin lines of cinnamon.

Chicken Stuffed with Couscous

SERVES 4

1 (3 pound 5-ounce) chicken

1 large red onion, grated

2 tablespoons honey

2 tablespoons butter

1½ teaspoons ground cinnamon

½ teaspoon ground ginger

pinch of saffron threads, crumbled

water, to cook chicken

COUSCOUS STUFFING

1 cup couscous

1 teaspoon salt

1 tablespoon olive oil

¾ cup raisins

boiling water, to cover raisins

2 tablespoons vegetable oil

1 cup blanched almonds

2 tablespoons butter

2 teaspoons superfine sugar

1 teaspoon ground cinnamon

salt and freshly ground black pepper

Preheat the oven 390°F.

To make the couscous stuffing, follow the preparation for traditional Moroccan couscous on page 54 using ½ cup salted water in step one and ¾ cup water and the olive oil in step two, or follow package instructions for instant couscous.

Place the raisins in a small bowl and cover with boiling water. Set aside for 10 minutes to plump. Drain. **>**

Heat the vegetable oil in a medium-sized fry pan over low–medium heat. Add the almonds and cook until golden. Drain on paper towels and coarsely chop.

Add the butter, almonds, raisins, sugar and cinnamon to the couscous and rub through using your fingers to separate the grains. Add salt and freshly ground black pepper.

Wash the chicken and the cavity thoroughly with cold running water and pat dry with paper towels. Stuff the cavity of the chicken with the prepared couscous. To prevent the stuffing from falling out, fold over the two flaps of skin and secure using toothpicks. Tie the legs together using kitchen string. (Place any excess couscous in a small baking pan and cover with aluminum foil to heat through in the oven 20 minutes before the chicken is ready.)

Combine the red onion, honey, butter and spices in a bowl. Spread this mixture over the bottom of a large baking dish. Place the chicken on top and pour in 1¼ cups water. Cover with aluminum foil and cook in the oven for 45 minutes. Uncover the chicken and return to the oven, basting occasionally, for an additional 45 minutes or until the juices run clear from the thickest part of the thigh when tested.

Sweet Tomato Chicken

SERVES 4

1 (3 pound 5-ounce) chicken

8 tablespoons butter, cubed

1 clove garlic, finely chopped

½ teaspoon ground ginger

¼ teaspoon freshly ground black
pepper

pinch of saffron threads, crumbled

½ teaspoon salt

1 large red onion, grated

15 medium-sized tomatoes, peeled,
deseeded and coarsely chopped

3 tablespoons honey

2 teaspoons ground cinnamon

2 tablespoons vegetable oil

^{2}/$_3$ cup blanched almonds

Wash the chicken and the cavity thoroughly with cold running water and pat dry with paper towels.

Combine the butter, garlic, spices and salt in a bowl. Rub over the chicken and inside the cavity. Put half of the red onion and tomatoes in the bottom of a large saucepan, big enough to hold the chicken. Place the chicken on top and cover with the remaining red onion and tomatoes. Cover and cook over low–medium heat for 1½ hours or until the juices run clear from the thickest part of the thigh when tested. Remove the chicken, transfer to a plate, cover and set aside to keep warm. ❯

Add the honey and cinnamon to the saucepan and cook over low heat, stirring occasionally, for 20–30 minutes, until all of the liquid has evaporated.

Heat the vegetable oil in a medium-sized fry pan over low–medium heat. Add the almonds and cook until golden brown. Remove using a slotted spoon, drain on paper towels and coarsely chop.

Return the chicken to the saucepan to heat through, turning to coat in the tomato sauce. Serve scattered with almonds.

Chicken Stuffed with Kefta

SERVES 4

1 (3 pound 5-ounce) chicken

2 tablespoons butter

½ teaspoon paprika

½ teaspoon salt

¼ teaspoon freshly ground black
    pepper

KEFTA STUFFING

2 tablespoons olive oil

1 large red onion, grated

1 clove garlic, finely chopped

1 teaspoon ground cumin

1 teaspoon paprika

¼ teaspoon freshly ground black
    pepper

¼ teaspoon salt

7 ounces coarsely ground beef

water, to prepare kefta

juice of ½ lemon

3 large eggs, lightly beaten

3 tablespoons finely chopped fresh
    flat-leaf parsley

To make the kefta stuffing, heat the olive oil in a large fry pan over low–medium heat. Add the red onion, garlic, spices and salt and sauté until softened and fragrant. Add the coarsely ground beef and cook, stirring to break up, for 5 minutes or until browned. Pour in ¼ cup water and lemon juice and bring to a boil. Simmer for 2 minutes or until the liquid has reduced by half. Pour in the eggs and cook, stirring, until set. Add the parsley and stir to combine. Remove from the heat and set aside to cool slightly.

Preheat the oven to 390°F.

Wash the chicken and the cavity thoroughly with cold running water and pat dry with paper towels.

Combine the butter, paprika, salt and freshly ground black pepper in a small bowl. Rub over the chicken and inside the cavity. Stuff the cavity of the chicken with the prepared kefta. To prevent the stuffing from falling out, fold over the two flaps of skin and secure using toothpicks. Tie the legs together using kitchen string.

Bake in the oven for 1½ hours, basting occasionally, until the juices run clear from the thickest part of the thigh when tested.

Roast Chicken with Preserved Lemons & Olives

SERVES 4

1 (3 pound 5-ounce) chicken

2 preserved lemons

10 tablespoons butter, softened

2 cloves garlic, crushed

1½ teaspoons ground ginger

¼ teaspoon ground turmeric

pinch of saffron threads, crumbled

salt and freshly ground black pepper

2 large onions, thickly sliced

¾ cup red or green olives

water, to cook chicken

Preheat the oven to 390°F.

Wash the chicken and the cavity thoroughly with cold running water and pat dry with paper towels. Stuff the cavity of the chicken with one of the preserved lemons and tie the legs together using kitchen string.

Discard the flesh of the remaining preserved lemon and finely chop the skin. Combine the preserved lemon skin, butter, garlic and spices in a small bowl. Rub the butter mixture over the chicken. Season with salt and freshly ground black pepper.

Place the chicken in a large baking dish. Scatter the onions and olives around the chicken and pour in 1½ cups water. Cover with aluminum foil and bake for 45 minutes. Uncover and cook, basting occasionally, for an additional 45 minutes, until the juices run clear from the thickest part of the thigh when tested.

Chicken Stuffed with Spiced Rice

SERVES 4

1 (3 pound 5-ounce) chicken

2 tablespoons olive oil

1 teaspoon paprika

salt and freshly ground black pepper

water, to cook chicken

RICE STUFFING

water, to cook rice

½ cup long-grain rice, rinsed

2 tablespoons olive oil

1 tablespoon butter

1 large red onion, finely chopped

2 cloves garlic, finely chopped

1½ teaspoons paprika

1 teaspoon ground cumin

¼ teaspoon ground turmeric

¼ teaspoon cayenne pepper

2 chicken livers, finely chopped

¼ cup finely chopped fresh
    flat-leaf parsley

juice of ½ lemon

salt and freshly ground black pepper

To make the rice stuffing, place a medium-sized saucepan of water on high heat and bring to a boil. Add the rice and cook for 10–15 minutes, until just tender.

Preheat the oven to 390°F.

Heat the olive oil and butter in a large fry pan over low–medium heat. Add the red onion, garlic and spices and cook until softened and fragrant. Add the chicken livers and cook for an additional 2–3 minutes, until golden. Combine the rice, parsley and lemon juice and season with salt and freshly ground black pepper.

Wash the chicken and the cavity thoroughly with cold running water and pat dry with paper towels. Stuff the cavity of the chicken with the prepared rice. To prevent the stuffing from falling out, fold over the two flaps of skin and secure using toothpicks. Tie the legs together using kitchen string.

Put the chicken in a large baking dish. Drizzle with the olive oil, sprinkle with the paprika and season with salt and freshly ground black pepper. Pour 1½ cups water into the baking dish. Cover with aluminum foil and bake for 45 minutes. Uncover and cook, basting occasionally, for an additional 45 minutes, until the juices run clear from the thickest part of the thigh when tested.

Chicken Stuffed with Almond Paste

1 (3 pound 5-ounce) chicken

1 tablespoon butter

½ teaspoon ground cinnamon

½ teaspoon ground ginger

½ teaspoon salt

¼ teaspoon freshly ground black
  pepper

pinch of saffron threads, crushed

1 large red onion, grated

2 tablespoons finely chopped fresh
  flat-leaf parsley

juice of ½ lemon

water, to cook chicken

ALMOND STUFFING

2 tablespoons vegetable oil

1⅓ cups blanched almonds

¼ cup superfine sugar

2 tablespoons butter

½ teaspoon ground cinnamon

Wash the chicken and the cavity thoroughly with cold running water and pat dry with paper towels.

Combine the butter, cinnamon, ginger, salt, freshly ground black pepper and saffron in a bowl. Rub over the chicken and inside the cavity. Combine the red onion and parsley and put in the bottom of a saucepan big enough to hold the chicken. Place the chicken on top and pour in the lemon juice and ¼ cup water. Cover and cook over low–medium heat for 45 minutes.

To prepare the almond stuffing, heat the vegetable oil in a medium-sized fry pan over low–medium heat. Add the almonds and cook until golden. Remove using a slotted spoon and drain on paper towels. Blend the almonds, superfine sugar, butter and cinnamon together in a food processor or blender to make a smooth paste.

Preheat the oven to 390°F.

Remove the chicken from the saucepan and place in a deep baking dish. Pour any remaining cooking liquid around and over the chicken. Stuff the chicken with the prepared almond paste, being careful not to burn yourself. To prevent the stuffing from falling out, fold over the two flaps of skin and secure using tooth-picks. Tie the legs together using kitchen string.

Bake in the oven for 30–45 minutes, basting occasionally, until the juices run clear from the thickest part of the thigh when tested.

Chicken Stuffed with Vermicelli

SERVES 4

1 (3 pound 5-ounce) chicken

1 large red onion, finely chopped

¼ cup olive oil

2 cloves garlic, finely chopped

½ teaspoon ground ginger

pinch of saffron threads

salt and freshly ground black pepper

water, to cook chicken

VERMICELLI STUFFING

3½ ounce vermicelli rice noodles

boiling water, to soak noodles

2 tablespoons olive oil

2 cloves garlic, crushed

1 teaspoon ground ginger

1 teaspoon ground cumin

½ teaspoon ground turmeric

2 tablespoons finely chopped fresh flat-leaf parsley

2 tablespoons finely chopped fresh cilantro

salt and freshly ground black pepper

Preheat the oven to 390°F.

To make the vermicelli stuffing, soak the vermicelli rice noodles in boiling water for 5 minutes, until softened. Drain and roughly chop. Combine the noodles, olive oil, garlic and spices in a bowl. Add the parsley and cilantro, mix and season with salt and freshly ground black pepper. >

Wash the chicken and the cavity thoroughly with cold running water and pat dry with paper towels. Stuff the cavity of the chicken with the prepared stuffing. To prevent the stuffing from falling out, fold over the two flaps of skin and secure using toothpicks. Tie the legs together using kitchen string.

Place the red onion in the bottom of a large baking dish and the chicken on top. Combine the olive oil, garlic, ginger and saffron in a small bowl. Pour over the chicken and rub to coat. Season with salt and freshly ground black pepper. Pour 1½ cups water into the baking dish. Cover with aluminum foil and cook in the oven for 45 minutes. Uncover the chicken and return to the oven to cook, basting occasionally, for an additional 45 minutes, until the juices run clear from the thickest part of the thigh when tested.

M'qualli-spiced Chicken

SERVES 4

1 (3 pound 5-ounce) chicken,
  butterflied

1 medium red onion, grated

¼ cup olive oil

2 tablespoons lemon juice

2 teaspoons ground ginger

1 preserved lemon, finely chopped

2 pinches saffron threads, crumbled

½ teaspoon salt

¼ teaspoon freshly ground black
  pepper

2 lemons, cut into wedges

Insert two metal skewers through the chicken, beginning at the thickest part of each breast and going all the way through to each thigh. This will make sure that the chicken stays spread open. Score the chicken in the thickest part of each leg to help it cook evenly.

Combine the remaining ingredients, except the lemon wedges, in a small bowl. Coat the chicken in this spice mixture and place in the refrigerator to marinate for at least 6 hours or overnight.

Preheat barbecue to medium–high. Cook the chicken, basting with the marinade, for 10–15 minutes on each side, until the juices run clear from the thickest part of each thigh when tested. Remove the skewers, then cut the chicken into portions and serve with lemon wedges.

Sweets

In Morocco, women traditionally do most of the cooking and culinary knowledge is passed down through the generations. Great pride is taken in what is prepared and sweet-making is no exception. Women gather together in each other's houses to make large batches of delicious pastries. A decadent bounty is always produced and divided at the end of the day, keeping households well stocked for visitors who may stop by.

Moroccan sweets and pastries are rarely eaten as part of a meal, except during the month of Ramadan and at celebrations or feasts. Instead they are enjoyed as afternoon treats. Platters of seasonal fresh fruit are traditionally served at the end of most meals.

< Doughnuts (page 174)

Doughnuts

Sfinges

MAKES 20

2 teaspoons dry yeast

1 teaspoon superfine sugar, plus extra
    for dusting (optional)

1 cup lukewarm water

2½ cups all-purpose flour

1 teaspoon salt

vegetable oil, for deep-frying

piece of bread, to test vegetable oil

Combine the yeast, superfine sugar and ¼ cup of the water in a small bowl. Cover with a clean kitchen towel and set aside in a warm place for 10 minutes or until the yeast begins to bubble.

Sift the all-purpose flour and salt into a bowl and make a well in the center. Pour in the yeast mixture and the remaining water and gradually stir into the flour to form a dough.

Knead the dough for 10–15 minutes, until the dough becomes, soft, loose and elastic. Place in a lightly-oiled bowl and cover with a clean kitchen towel. Put in a warm place for 1 hour or until doubled in size.

Punch out the dough to remove all the air. Divide into 20 even-sized balls and place on a lightly-oiled baking sheet. Using your index finger, make a hole in the center of one of the balls and swing the dough around your finger to make a large, loose ring. Swing and stretch the dough until you can fit your three middle fingers in the center. Lay the dough ring on another lightly-oiled baking sheet. Repeat with the remaining dough. Cover with a clean kitchen towel and set aside in a warm place for 20 minutes or until doubled in size.

Fill a large, heavy-based saucepan half-full with vegetable oil for deep-frying. Heat the vegetable oil to 360°F or until a piece of bread browns in 15 seconds when tested.

Carefully drop the rings, a few at a time, into the vegetable oil and deep-fry in batches, turning occasionally, until puffed and golden brown. Remove using a slotted spoon and drain on paper towels.

Serve immediately, sprinkled with superfine sugar (if using).

Almond Batons

MAKES 25

1 egg white, lightly beaten

¼ cup sesame seeds

PASTRY

½ cup all-purpose flour

2 teaspoons confectioner's (powdered) sugar

pinch of salt

¼ cup heavy cream

ALMOND FILLING

¾ cup ground almonds

⅓ cup confectioner's (powdered) sugar

½ teaspoon ground cinnamon

2 teaspoons softened butter

1 tablespoon orange-blossom water

To make the pastry, combine the all-purpose flour, confectioner's sugar and salt in a medium-sized bowl. Add the heavy cream and stir to combine. Knead to make a dough. Wrap in food wrap and refrigerate for 30 minutes.

Preheat the oven to 340°F. Line a baking sheet with parchment (baking) paper.

For the almond filling, combine ground almonds, confectioner's sugar and cinnamon. Add butter and orange-blossom water, and knead to a paste. Roll into ⅜-inch thick logs.

Roll the pastry out to ⅛-inch thick. Place a log of filling on the pastry, wrap to enclose and press to seal. Repeat with the remaining filling and pastry. Cut into 2-inch batons. Dip the ends in egg white, then sesame seeds. Bake for 15–20 minutes, until just cooked but still pale in color.

Honeyed Pastry Ribbons

Chebbakia

MAKES 25

vegetable oil, for deep-frying and
  baking sheet

piece of bread, to test vegetable oil

¼ cup sesame seeds, toasted

PASTRY

¾ cup sesame seeds, toasted

1 teaspoon dry yeast

pinch of saffron threads, finely
  crushed

3 tablespoons lukewarm water

2 cups all-purpose flour

½ teaspoon ground cinnamon

pinch of salt

2 tablespoons olive oil

2 tablespoons butter, melted

1½ tablespoons white-wine vinegar

1 large egg, lightly beaten

2 tablespoons orange-blossom water

HONEY DIP

2 cups honey

3 tablespoons orange-blossom water

To make the pastry, place the sesame seeds in a food processor or blender and finely grind to a flour-like consistency. Mix the yeast, saffron and water in a small bowl and set aside.

Lightly oil a baking sheet.

Combine the ground sesame seeds, all-purpose flour, cinnamon and salt in a medium-sized bowl. Make a well in the center and add the olive oil, butter, white-wine vinegar and egg. Rub the mixture together using your fingertips to create a fine texture, resembling breadcrumbs. Add the yeast mixture and the orange-blossom water, mixing until a dough forms. **>**

Knead for 10–15 minutes, or until it becomes elastic. Divide the dough into five even-sized balls and place on the baking sheet. Loosely cover with food wrap and set aside to rest in a warm place for 20 minutes.

Lightly flour a clean counter top and roll out a portion of dough to less than ¼-inch thick. Cut out 4-inch squares using a fluted pastry wheel. Make four cuts the same length across the center of each square, leaving a ⅝-inch border, to create five even strips connected down two edges.

To shape the ribbons, gently hold the first, third and fifth strips with your fingers and lift the pastry square off the counter top, allowing the remaining two strips to hang down. Press the two side corners closest to you together firmly to secure, and to prevent them from coming apart when cooking. Feed the pressed corners up through the center hole you have created between the strips (almost as if you are turning the chebbakia inside out to create a flower-like shape). Place on the lightly-oiled baking sheet and set aside. Any pastry scraps can be re-kneaded and re-rolled once to create additional pastries.

To make the honey dip, pour the honey and orange-blossom water into a large fry pan and warm over low heat. If the honey gets too hot and begins to boil, add a little additional orange-blossom water and reduce the temperature slightly.

Pour enough vegetable oil into a large fry pan for deep-frying. Heat to 360°F or until a piece of bread browns in 15 seconds when tested.

Deep-fry the pastries in batches for 3 minutes on each side, until golden brown and crisp. Remove each batch using a slotted spoon, drain for a few seconds, then place directly in the prepared honey dip. Hold the pastries down in the honey for 1 minute and turn until fully coated. Let the pastries soak up the honey for 2–3 minutes. Remove using a slotted spoon, drain slightly and place on a baking sheet. Sprinkle immediately with the toasted sesame seeds.

❁ Chebbakia can be found everywhere in Morocco during the month of Ramadan. They are traditionally eaten alongside harira soup (page 32) to break the fast after the sun has set.

❁ Chebbakia and other Moroccan pastries are usually made in bulk with the help of many women, either family members or neighbors, and then divided up to share. Although it is possible to make and shape the chebbakia on your own, it is recommended that you have help for the final stages of frying and dipping in honey as the transferring needs to be done quickly for optimum results.

Almond Briouats

MAKES 30

2 pounds ground almonds

¼ cup superfine sugar

7 tablespoons butter, softened

⅓ cup orange-blossom water

½ teaspoon ground cinnamon

10 large spring-roll wrappers

2 large egg yolks, lightly beaten

vegetable oil, for deep-frying

piece of bread, to test vegetable oil

HONEY DIP

2 cups honey

3 tablespoons orange-blossom water

In a medium-sized bowl, combine the ground almonds, superfine sugar, butter, orange-blossom water and cinnamon. Knead, then roll the mixture into 30 even-sized balls.

Place a spring-roll wrapper on a clean counter top and cut into three even lengths. Place a ball of filling at the end of each length and flatten slightly. Enclose the filling in the spring-roll wrapper, folding the spring-roll wrapper back and forth and flattening each time, to create a triangular bundle. Brush the ends with egg yolk and press to seal. Repeat the process with the remaining filling and spring-roll wrappers.

Pour enough vegetable oil into a large fry pan for deep-frying. Heat to 360°F or until a piece of bread browns in 15 seconds when tested. **>**

To make the honey dip, pour the honey and orange-blossom water into a large fry pan and warm over low heat. If the honey gets too hot and begins to boil, add a little additional orange-blossom water and reduce the temperature slightly.

Deep-fry the briouats in batches for 1–2 minutes on each side, until golden brown and crisp. Remove using a slotted spoon, drain for a few seconds and place directly in the prepared honey dip. Hold down in the honey for 1 minute and turn until fully coated. Let the pastries soak up the honey for 3–5 minutes. Remove using a slotted spoon, allowing excess honey to drain, and place on a baking sheet.

�֍ Briouats are small, stuffed, crispy pastries. They can be prepared up to the cooking stage and frozen in an airtight container for up to 2–3 months.

Almond-filled Pastry Snake

M'hanncha

MAKES 1 LARGE SNAKE

9 sheets filo pastry

3 tablespoons butter, melted

1 egg yolk

water, to brush pastry

1 tablespoon coarsely chopped slivered
  almonds

ALMOND FILLING

1¹/³ cup ground almonds

¾ cup confectioner's (powdered)
  sugar

1 teaspoon ground cinnamon

2 tablespoons orange-blossom water

1½ tablespoons butter, melted

HONEY SYRUP

2 tablespoons honey, warmed

1 tablespoon orange-blossom water

To make the almond filling, combine the ground almonds, confectioner's (powdered) sugar and cinnamon in a bowl. Add the orange-blossom water and butter and stir to combine. Divide the filling into three even-sized portions and shape into logs, slightly shorter than the width of a sheet of filo pastry.

Preheat the oven to 360°F. Line a baking sheet with parchment (baking) paper.

Lay a sheet of filo pastry on a clean counter top and brush with melted butter. Add another two layers of filo pastry, brushing with butter in between each layer. Keep the remaining filo pastry covered with a damp, clean kitchen towel to prevent it from drying out. **>**

Place a stick of filling across the long edge of the prepared filo pastry and roll up loosely to enclose the filling. Repeat the process with the remaining filling and filo pastry sheets.

Place one filled pastry bundle on the prepared baking sheet seam-side down and curl into a tight spiral, pinching the center end closed. Wrap the remaining filled pastry bundles, one at a time, around the spiral, joining the ends together, to create a coiled snake. Brush the top with the remaining melted butter.

Combine the egg yolk and 1 tablespoon water in a cup and brush over the top of the pastry coil. Sprinkle with the slivered almonds and bake in the oven for 30–35 minutes or until crisp and golden brown.

To make the honey syrup, heat the honey and orange-blossom water together in a small saucepan.

Remove the pastry snake from the oven and brush with the honey syrup. Set aside to cool slightly.

Serve warm or at room temperature.

Gazelle's Horns

MAKES 36

ALMOND FILLING	PASTRY
13½ ounces ground almonds	1½ cups all-purpose flour
½ cup confectioner's (powdered) sugar	2 tablespoons confectioner's (powdered) sugar, plus extra for dusting (optional)
1 teaspoon ground cinnamon	
2 tablespoons unsalted butter, melted and cooled	2 tablespoons butter, melted
	water, to prepare dough
1 tablespoon orange-blossom water	2 tablespoons orange-blossom water

To make the almond filling, combine the ground almonds, confectioner's (powdered) sugar and cinnamon in a small bowl. Add the butter and orange-blossom water and stir to combine. Divide the filling into four and place in the refrigerator for 10 minutes to cool.

To make the pastry, sift the all-purpose flour and confectioner's (powdered) sugar into a bowl. Pour in the butter, then gradually pour in ⅓ cup water and the orange-blossom water, stirring until a sticky dough begins to form. Knead the dough, punching into it with your fists for 15–20 minutes, until it is smooth and elastic and comes away from the bowl easily. Divide into four, then shape into blocks and refrigerate for 10 minutes. >

Preheat the oven to 300°F. Line a baking sheet with parchment (baking) paper.

Divide each portion of almond filling into 9 even-sized balls, then shape into tapered logs and set aside.

Roll out one portion of dough to make a long 4-inch wide strip. Lay a log of almond filling across the shortest end of the dough, leaving a 2-inch border. Moisten around the filling with water. Fold the pastry over to enclose the filling, pressing with your fingers to seal. Cut around the edge, gently shape into a crescent and place on the prepared baking sheet. Make a few holes in the top using a toothpick to prevent the pastry from cracking. Repeat the process with the remaining dough and almond filling.

Bake in the oven for 10–15 minutes, until just cooked but still pale in color. Transfer to a wire rack to cool completely. Dust with confectioner's (powdered) sugar (if using).

Crisp Almond & Cream Layers

Keneffa

SERVES 4–6

vegetable oil, for deep-frying	CRÈME PÂTISSIÈRE
piece of bread, to test vegetable oil	10 quarts milk
1 cup whole blanched almonds	1 vanilla bean, split in half lengthwise
9 spring-roll wrappers	and seeds scraped
¼ cup superfine sugar	4 large egg yolks
finely chopped almonds, to sprinkle	¼ cup superfine sugar
	2 tablespoons all-purpose flour
	1 tablespoon rosewater

To make the crème patissière, place the milk and vanilla bean and seeds in a medium-sized saucepan and bring to just below the boiling point. Remove from the heat and set aside.

Beat the egg yolks and sugar together in a medium-sized bowl using an electric mixer, until pale and thick. Stir in the all-purpose flour. Gradually add the hot milk, mixture, stirring with a wooden spoon to incorporate. Return to the pan and cook over low–medium heat, stirring continuously, until thickened enough to coat the back of the spoon. Discard the vanilla bean and stir in the rosewater. Take off the heat, cover with a piece of parchment (baking) paper to prevent a skin from forming and set aside to cool slightly. ❯

Pour enough vegetable oil into a large fry pan for deep-frying. Heat the vegetable oil to 360°F or until a piece of bread browns in 15 seconds when tested.

Deep-fry the almonds for 2 minutes or until golden brown. Remove using a slotted spoon and place on paper towels to drain and cool.

Cut the spring-roll wrappers into 8-inch rounds. Deep-fry until golden brown and crisp. Remove from the vegetable oil and drain on paper towels.

Blend the almonds and superfine sugar in a food processor or blender until coarsely chopped.

To assemble, arrange three spring-roll rounds on a large serving plate. Sprinkle with one-third of the almond mixture. Thin the crème patissière with a little warm milk if necessary and pour a layer over the top. Cover with another three spring-roll rounds and repeat the process, finishing with a sprinkling of finely chopped almonds on top. Serve any remaining crème patissière on the side.

❋ Keneffa refers to crispy pastry sheets made with different cream fiillings. They are a common Moroccan treat.

Sesame Biscuits

Ghoriba behla

MAKES 30

¼ cup sesame seeds, toasted

1¾ cups all-purpose flour

¹/₃ cup confectioner's (powdered) sugar

½ teaspoon dry yeast

pinch of salt

7 tablespoons butter, melted

¼ cup vegetable oil

½ teaspoon vanilla extract

Preheat the oven to 340°F. Line a baking sheet with parchment (baking) paper.

Place the sesame seeds in a food processor or blender and finely grind. Combine with the all-purpose flour, confectioner's (powdered) sugar, yeast and salt in a medium-sized bowl. Add the butter, vegetable oil and vanilla and rub together using your fingertips to create a fine texture resembling breadcrumbs. Squeeze golfball-sized portions of the mixture in the palm of your hand to bind the mixture together. Gently roll into balls. Transfer the balls back and forth from one palm to the other to flatten slightly. (The mixture is quite crumbly and it can take a little practice to shape.)

Place the shaped dough on the prepared baking sheet and bake in the oven for 15 minutes or until golden brown. Let cool on the baking sheet for 10 minutes, then transfer to a wire rack to cool completely.

Date Crescents

MAKES 20

1 large egg white, lightly beaten

confectioner's (powdered) sugar, for dusting

PASTRY

3^{1}/$_{3}$ cups all-purpose flour

¼ cup confectioner's (powdered) sugar

2¼ sticks (18 tablespoons) butter, cubed

^{1}/$_{3}$ cup milk

DATE FILLING

1 pound 2 ounces pitted dried dates

boiling water, to soak and cook dates

1 tablespoon ground almonds

1 tablespoon orange-blossom water

2 teaspoons butter

1 teaspoon ground cinnamon

To make the pastry, sift the all-purpose flour and confectioner's (powdered) sugar together into a medium-sized bowl. Rub in the butter, using your fingertips, until the mixture resembles fine breadcrumbs. Add the milk, a little at a time, until a dough forms. Shape into a ball, cover with food wrap and refrigerate for 30 minutes.

To make the date filling, place the dates in a small saucepan and cover with ½ cup boiling water. Set aside to soak for 10 minutes or until softened. Add an additional ¼ cup water and cook, stirring, over low heat for 10 minutes or until a paste forms. Add the ground almonds, orange-blossom water, butter and cinnamon and stir to combine. Transfer to a small bowl and set aside to cool. **>**

Preheat the oven to 320°F. Line 2 baking sheets with parchment (baking) paper.

Roll the pastry out to ⅛-inch thick on a lightly-floured, clean counter top. Cut out rounds using an 3-inch pastry cutter. Brush the edges of one of the pastry rounds with egg white and place a small ball of date filling in the center of the pastry round. Fold the pastry round in half to enclose the filling and create a crescent shape. Press the curved edge with your finger tips to seal and place on the prepared baking sheet. Repeat with remaining pastry rounds and date filling

Lightly brush the top of the crescents with egg white and bake in the oven for 15–20 minutes, until just golden. Transfer to a wire rack to cool.

Dust thoroughly with confectioner's sugar and serve.

Almond Biscuits

Ghoriba

MAKES 40

1¼ cups confectioner's (powdered) sugar, plus extra for dipping

1½ teaspoons baking powder

1 teaspoon ground cinnamon

13½ ounces ground almonds

3 large eggs, separated

1 tablespoon butter, softened

finely grated zest of ½ lemon

Preheat the oven to 340°F. Lightly grease a baking sheet.

Sift the confectioner's (powdered) sugar, baking powder and cinnamon together into a medium-sized bowl. Add the ground almonds and stir to combine.

Add the egg yolks, butter and lemon zest and stir to form a dough. Roll the dough into 40 even-sized balls and flatten slightly.

Lightly beat the egg whites in a small bowl. Dip the flattened balls in egg whites followed by confectioner's (powdered) sugar to coat.

Arrange the flattened balls ¾-inch apart on the prepared backing sheet and bake in the oven for 15 minutes or until golden brown. Let cool on the baking sheet for 10 minutes, then transfer to a wire rack to cool completely.

Macaroons

MAKES 20

2½ cups whole almonds, plus 20 extra to decorate

1 cup confectioner's (powdered) sugar

1 teaspoon baking powder

½ teaspoon ground cinnamon

2 large eggs, separated

finely grated zest of ½ lemon

Preheat the oven to 360°F. Line a baking tray with parchment (baking) paper.

Place the almonds in a food processor or blender and blend until finely ground.

Combine the ground almonds, confectioner's (powdered) sugar, baking powder and cinnamon in a bowl. Add the egg yolks and lemon zest and rub together with your fingers to create a crumb-like texture.

Whip the egg whites in a bowl to form soft peaks. Add to the almond mixture and fold in gently to combine.

Shape the mixture into 20 even-sized balls. Arrange the macaroons roughly ¾ inches apart on the prepared baking sheet. Press an almond in the center of each macaroon and flatten slightly. Bake in the oven for 15 minutes or until golden brown. Let cool on the baking sheet for 10 minutes, then transfer to a wire rack to cool completely.

Moroccan Biscotti

Fekkas

MAKES ABOUT 60

2½ cups all-purpose flour

1 tablespoon baking powder

1 teaspoon ground cinnamon

1 cup superfine sugar

3 large eggs

10 sticks (13 tablespoons) butter, melted

1 cup whole almonds, coarsely chopped

½ cup raisins

3 tablespoons sesame seeds

1 large egg white, lightly beaten

Preheat the oven to 360°F. Line a baking sheet with parchment (baking) paper.

Sift the all-purpose flour, baking powder and cinnamon into a bowl.

Whisk the superfine sugar and eggs together. Add the butter, almonds, raisins and sesame seeds and stir to combine. Gradually add the all-purpose flour, stirring until a dough begins to form. Shape into two even-sized sticks 2-inches wide. Transfer the logs to the prepared baking sheet and brush the tops with egg white. Bake for 20 minutes or until golden brown and firm to the touch.

Remove from the oven and set aside to cool for 20 minutes. Cut the logs, using a sharp serrated knife, into ⅜-inch thick slices. Return the slices to the baking sheet and bake for 10–15 minutes or until crisp and golden brown. Remove from the oven and transfer to a wire rack to cool completely.

Semolina Biscuits with Dates

Makrout

MAKES 30

vegetable oil, for deep-frying

piece of bread, to test vegetable oil

DATE FILLING

½ pound pitted dried dates

water, to cook dates

1 tablespoon butter

1 tablespoon orange-blossom water

1 teaspoon ground cinnamon

DOUGH

1 cup coarse semolina

1 cup fine semolina (durum wheat)

1 tablespoon superfine sugar

pinch of salt

10 tablespoons butter, melted

¼ cup orange-blossom water

water, to form dough

HONEY DIP

1½ cups honey

1½ tablespoons orange-blossom water

To make the date filling, place the dates in a small saucepan with ¼ cup water. Cover and cook over very low heat for 10 minutes, until softened. Set aside and allow to cool. Add the butter, orange-blossom water and cinnamon and stir to make a paste.

To make the dough, combine the coarse and fine semolinas, superfine sugar and salt in a bowl. Add the butter, orange-blossom water and ⅓ cup water and knead to form a dough. Shape the dough into a stick. Make an incision down the center line but not all the way through, leaving the stick intact.

Shape the date filling into a stick the same length as the dough stick. Place the date stick inside the incision and enclose in the dough, pressing to seal. Score the top of the dough stick in a decorative crisscross pattern and cut into ¾-inch slices.

To make the honey dip, pour the honey and orange-blossom water into a medium-sized saucepan and warm over low heat.

Pour enough vegetable oil into a large fry pan for deep-frying. Heat vegetable oil to 360°F or until a piece of bread browns in 15 seconds when tested.

Deep-fry the biscuits in batches for 1–2 minutes on each side, until golden brown and crisp. Remove using a slotted spoon, drain for a few seconds and place directly in the prepared honey dip. Hold down in the honey for 1 minute and turn until fully coated. Let the biscuits soak up the honey for 1–2 minutes. Remove using a slotted spoon, allowing excess honey to drain. Place on a baking sheet and set aside to cool.

Almond and Chocolate Slice

Zelliges

MAKES 32

1 pound 3 ounces dark chocolate

water, to melt chocolate

8 ounces ground almonds

½ cup confectioner's (powdered)
  sugar

5½ tablespoons butter, softened

1¾ ounces white chocolate

Line a 11-inch × 7-inch baking sheet with parchment (baking) paper.

Place the dark chocolate in a bowl and melt over a small saucepan of barely simmering water, stirring until smooth. Pour half of the chocolate into the prepared baking sheet and, using a palate knife, spread out to an even layer. Refrigerate for 15–20 minutes, or until almost set.

Combine the ground almonds, confectioner's (powdered) sugar and butter in a bowl to form a paste. Roll out on a clean counter top, lightly dusted with confectioner's sugar, to a size to fit the chocolate-lined baking sheet. Cut the almond paste into six large squares and lay over the chocolate base. Pour over the remaining dark chocolate and spread to create a smooth, even surface.

Melt the white chocolate using the method above. Drizzle back and forth over the dark chocolate to create a decorative pattern. Refrigerate for 15–20 minutes or until almost set. Mark the surface into 32 portions and refrigerate until set. Cut into portions using a hot knife.

Sweet Couscous

SERVES 6

1½ cups couscous

water, to prepare and cook couscous

1½ teaspoons salt

2 tablespoons vegetable oil

1 cup whole blanched almonds

½ cup raisins

6 tablespoons butter

½ cup confectioner's (powdered)
  sugar, plus extra, to serve (optional)

1 tablespoon ground cinnamon

chilled milk, to serve (optional)

Place the couscous in a large, wide-based baking pan or bowl. Combine 3 cups water with the salt. Sprinkle 1 cup of the salted water over the couscous, rubbing it through and separating the grains with your fingers. Set aside for 10 minutes to allow the grains to swell with the water and dry out a little.

Fill the bottom of a steamer saucepan with water and bring to a boil. Rub your fingers through the couscous again, separating the grains. Place the couscous in the top of the steamer pan and set over the boiling water, making sure that the top steamer section is not touching the water. When steam begins to rise through the couscous, steam for an additional 10 minutes. Turn the couscous out onto a baking pan. Sprinkle with another 1 cup salted water and rub through the couscous, separating the grains with your fingers. Set aside for 10 minutes to swell and dry out a little. **>**

Heat the vegetable oil in a medium-sized fry pan over low–medium heat. Add the almonds and cook until golden brown. Remove using a slotted spoon, drain on paper towels and coarsely chop.

Separate the couscous grains again using your fingers and return to the top of the steamer. When the steam begins to rise through the couscous, steam for an additional 10 minutes. Place the couscous back onto the baking pan. Add the raisins and half of the butter, and sprinkle with the remaining salted water. Rub through the couscous, separating the grains with your fingers. Set aside for 10 minutes to swell and dry out a little.

Return the couscous to the steamer pan for one final steaming of 10 minutes. Place the couscous back onto the baking pan, add the remaining butter and mix through using your fingers to separate the grains.

Pile the couscous onto a serving dish to form a dome. To decorate, scatter with almonds and create alternate lines of confectioner's sugar and cinnamon coming down from the center point.

Sprinkle with additional confectioner's (powdered) sugar if desired. May serve with chilled milk.

Moroccan Rice Pudding

SERVES 6–8

1¹/₃ cups short-grain rice

¹/₃ cup granulated white sugar, plus
   extra to serve (optional)

½ teaspoon salt

water, to cook rice

1¼ quarts milk

1 cinnamon stick

3 tablespoons butter

2 tablespoons orange-blossom water

2 teaspoons ground cinnamon

chilled milk, to serve (optional)

Place the short-grain rice, granulated white sugar and salt in a medium-sized saucepan with 2½ cups water and bring to a boil. Decrease the heat to low and cook, stirring occasionally, until the water has been absorbed.

Add half of the milk, the cinnamon stick and half of the butter. Continue cooking on low, stirring occasionally to prevent the rice from sticking, until all the liquid has been absorbed. Gradually add the remaining milk, stirring until the rice is cooked and swollen and creamy in texture. Add the orange-blossom water. **>**

Spoon the rice onto a serving plate to form a dome shape. Decorate with lines of ground cinnamon coming down from the center and dot with the remaining butter.

Sprinkle with additional granulated white sugar (if desired). May serve with chilled milk.

Sesame Brittle

MAKES 30

1 cup superfine sugar

1 cup sesame seeds, toasted

Place the superfine sugar in a small saucepan over low heat. Heat until it begins to melt and turn golden. Swirl the sugar around so that it colors evenly, but do not stir. When it turns a light golden color, add the sesame seeds, swirling to combine and evenly distribute.

Pour out onto an oiled marble or metal surface. Using a lightly-oiled rolling pin or metal spoon, spread out the sesame-sugar mixture to make a ¼-inch thick square. Work quickly or the sesame-sugar mixture will harden. Set aside for 5 minutes to harden completely.

Cut into approximately 30 squares.

Store in a dry airtight container for up to 2 weeks.

❋ When liquid, the sesame-sugar mixture is considered to be toffee; once hardened, it is considered brittle.

Stuffed Dates

3 ounces ground almonds

2 tablespoons confectioner's
(powdered) sugar

½ teaspoon ground cinnamon

2 teaspoons orange-blossom water

few drops of green food coloring

few drops of pink food coloring

20 fresh dates, pitted

superfine sugar, for sprinkling

Combine the ground almonds, confectioner's (powdered) sugar and cinnamon in a small bowl. Gradually add the orange-blossom water and blend to create a paste. Divide the paste in half.

Tint half of the paste pale green and the other half pale pink, adding a few drops at a time of the appropriate food coloring and stirring to combine.

Shape the filling into small rounded logs and stuff inside the dates. Sprinkle with superfine sugar and arrange on a serving plate.

Sesame, Almond & Honey Cone

Slelou

MAKES 2 CUPS

2¹/₃ cups all-purpose flour

2 cups whole blanched almonds

8½ ounces sesame seeds

2 sticks (16 tablespoons) butter, melted

3 tablespoons honey

½ cup confectioner's (powdered)

sugar, plus extra for dusting

2 teaspoons ground cinnamon

1 teaspoon ground aniseed

¼ teaspoon ground nutmeg

2 tablespoons vegetable oil

Toast the all-purpose flour in a dry fry pan over low heat, stirring constantly, until golden brown. Transfer to a medium-sized bowl and set aside to cool.

Toast 1½ cups almonds and the sesame seeds in the same fry pan, over low heat, until golden brown. Set aside to cool.

Melt the butter and honey together in a small saucepan over low heat. Set aside to cool slightly.

Transfer the almonds and sesame seeds to a food processor or blender and blend to a fine powder. Add the toasted all-purpose flour, confectioner's (powdered) sugar, cinnamon, aniseed and nutmeg and blend until combined. Transfer to a medium-sized bowl. Pour in the honey and butter mixture and stir to combine. **>**

Heat the vegetable oil in a medium-sized fry pan over low heat. Add the remaining almonds and fry until golden. Remove using a slotted spoon, drain on paper towels and set aside to cool.

Pile the almond and sesame seed mixture into a cone shape on a serving plate and dust heavily with confectioner's (powdered) sugar. Decorate with the whole almonds, creating three or four lines coming down from the center point.

❖ Slelou is served as a celebratory dish at weddings and after a child has been born. It is also offered during Ramadan to restore energy and provide nourishment. Slelou is traditionally eaten communally with teaspoons.

❖ Instead of making a cone shape with the mixture, add 2 extra tablespoons of honey and shape the mixture into small balls. Roll in confectioner's (powdered) sugar and decorate each ball with half of a toasted almond.

Fresh Figs with Honey
& Toasted Almonds

SERVES 4

2 tablespoons sliced almonds

8 ripe fresh figs

1 tablespoon fragrant light honey
   (such as clover or alfalfa)

Preheat a broiler to medium–high.

Spread the almonds over a baking sheet and toast under the broiler until golden.

Cut the figs in half lengthwise and arrange on a serving plate. Drizzle with the honey and scatter with the toasted almonds.

Serve immediately.

Cinnamon-spiced Orange Slices

SERVES 4

4 oranges

1 tablespoon orange-blossom water

1 teaspoon ground cinnamon

Peel the oranges using a small sharp knife and cut away the pith (soft, white fibrous tissue). Slice the oranges into rounds, removing any seeds.

Arrange the orange slices on a serving plate. Drizzle with the orange-blossom water and sprinkle with the cinnamon.

Serve immediately.

Melon & Mint Salad

SERVES 4–6

¼ small watermelon

¼ honeydew melon

¼ cantaloupe melon

3 tablespoons finely chopped fresh
   mint

Remove and discard the skin of the watermelon and cut into 1½-inch cubes. Remove and discard any visible seeds.

Remove and discard the skins off the honeydew and cantaloupe melons, scoop out and discard the seeds and cut into 1½-inch cubes.

Place all of the melon cubes and mint in a large bowl and toss to combine.

Serve immediately.

Breads, Drinks
& Extras

Moroccan cuisine would not be the same without the delicious extras that follow. Try making Moroccan bread so you can eat tagine the traditional way, with your right hand, soaking up the juices. And with your own preserved lemons, harissa, ras el hanout and marinated olives in the kitchen, you'll never be short of ways to add flavor to tagines, fish and meat dishes.

A traditional Moroccan breakfast is a great way to start the day. Recipes here include harchas (semolina flatbread), m'smmens (crêpes) and beghrir (semolina pancakes) topped with amalou (almond and honey spread), jam, or melted butter and fragrant honey.

Sweetened mint tea is a part of daily life in Morocco. It is served after most meals, sipped throughout the day, shared as a part of making business deals and always made when visitors stop by. Prepared before you in ceremonial fashion, the tea is boiled, poured, discarded and re-poured into small, intricately decorated glasses.

< Semolina Flatbread (page 222)

Semolina Flatbread

Harchas

MAKES 1

1½ cups fine semolina, plus extra for
  sprinkling

1 tablespoon superfine sugar

1 teaspoon baking powder

½ teaspoon salt

1 cup milk

butter and honey, jam or amaloou
  (to serve)

Combine the fine semolina, superfine sugar, baking powder and salt in a medium-sized bowl. Add the milk, stir to combine and set aside for 5 minutes.

Preheat a medium-sized non-stick fry pan over low–medium heat. Sprinkle the pan with fine semolina. Spoon the mixture into the pan and press down flat using a wet hand. Sprinkle with fine semolina and cook for 3–5 minutes on each side until golden brown.

Cut in half horizontally around the circumference (as you would an English muffin or bagel).

Serve warm with butter and honey, jam or amalou (almond & honey spread, page 230).

Moroccan Crêpes

M'smmens

MAKES 8

5½ ounces fine semolina, plus extra
   for sprinkling

3 cups all-purpose flour

2 teaspoons baking powder

2 tablespoons superfine sugar

1 teaspoon salt

water, to prepare dough

9 tablespoons unsalted butter

vegetable oil, for frying

butter and honey, jam or amaloou
   (to serve)

Sift the fine semolina, all-purpose flour, baking powder, superfine sugar and salt into a medium-sized bowl. Gradually add 1 cup water, stirring to combine until a dough begins to form. Knead the dough for 10 minutes or until a smooth, elastic ball is formed. Set aside for 10 minutes to rest.

Melt the butter in a small saucepan over low heat and set aside.

Using lightly-oiled hands, shape the dough into eight balls, approximately twice the size of golfballs. Flatten the balls out one at a time into 6-inch rounds. Drizzle with melted butter and lightly sprinkle with fine semolina. Fold the edges into the center, overlapping to make a rectangle. Half-turn and fold the edges in again, overlapping to make a small square bundle. Set aside to rest for 10 minutes. >

Flatten each bundle of dough into a square about the size of your hand.

Heat a medium-sized fry pan over medium–high heat. Drizzle with vegetable oil and cook the dough squares for 10 seconds on each side to seal. Cook for an additional 1–2 minutes on each side, until golden.

Serve hot with butter and honey, jam or amalou (page 230).

❄ M'smmens are a traditional Moroccan breakfast food.

Moroccan Bread

MAKES 3 (4-IN) ROUND LOAVES

2½ cups all-purpose flour

1 cup whole wheat flour

2 teaspoons salt

1 tablespoon dry yeast

1 tablespoon granulated white sugar

1¼ cups lukewarm water

vegetable oil, to prepare baking sheets

fine semolina, for sprinkling

Sift the all-purpose and whole wheat flours and salt together into a large bowl and make a well in the center. Place the yeast and granulated white sugar in the well. Pour ½ cup water into the well, mixing with the yeast to combine. Gradually add the remaining water and stir in the flour mixture until a dough begins to form.

Knead the dough for 10–15 minutes, adding a little extra water or flour if necessary, to make a smooth, elastic dough. Divide the dough into three equal-sized balls and place on a lightly-greased baking sheet. Cover with a clean kitchen towel and put in a warm place for 30–45 minutes, until doubled in size.

Preheat the oven to 390°F–420°F. Lightly oil 2 large baking sheets and sprinkle with fine semolina. ❯

Using the palm of your hand, press and flatten the balls to 4-inch rounds. Sprinkle the tops with fine semolina and transfer to the prepared baking sheets. Bake in the oven for 15–20 minutes or until golden brown. When the bread is cooked it will sound hollow when tapped on the bottom.

❈ Bread is eaten at almost every Moroccan meal. It is used to soak up the juices of tagine and to scoop tasty morsels into your mouth.

❈ As this bread contains no preservatives, it is best eaten on the day it is made.

Semolina Pancakes

Beghrir

MAKES 30

3½ cups lukewarm water

2½ teaspoons dry yeast

1 pound 5 ounces fine semolina

¾ cup all-purpose flour

1 tablespoon baking powder

2 teaspoons salt

1 tablespoon orange-blossom water

butter and honey, jam or amaloou
    (to serve)

Combine ⅓ cup water and the yeast in a small bowl.

Sift the fine semolina, all-purpose flour, baking powder and salt into a large bowl. Make a well in the dry ingredients and add the yeast mixture, remaining water and orange-blossom water, and stir to combine.

Pour the semolina mixture into a food processor or blender and blend for 2–3 minutes, to create a smooth, cream-like consistency. Transfer to a large bowl, cover with a clean kitchen towel and set aside in a warm place for 20–30 minutes, until bubbly.

Preheat a small non-stick fry pan over medium–high heat. Pour a small ladleful of batter into the pan and slightly rotate the pan to create an even round pancake. Turn the heat down to medium and cook the pancake on one side for 1–2 minutes, until the bubbles have popped and the pancake has cooked through. Remove the pancake from the pan using a pancake flipper and set aside under a clean kitchen towel to keep warm.

Repeat with the remaining mixture.

Serve warm with butter and honey, jam or amalou (page 230).

✳ Beghrir are a traditional Moroccan breakfast food. They can be frounceen for future use.

Almond & Honey Spread

Amalou

MAKES ABOUT 1 CUP

6 ounces ground almonds

$^1/_3$ cup walnut or vegetable oil

3 tablespoons honey

Place the ground almonds in a large fry pan over low–medium heat and toast for 4–5 minutes, until golden brown. Combine with the walnut or vegetable oil and honey in a small bowl and mix well. Add more honey for sweetness, if desired.

❊ Serve amalou with Moroccan bread (page 225), beghrir (page 228) or m'smmens (page 223).

❊ Amalou will keep in a sealed jar in the refrigerator for 2–3 weeks.

Broad Bean (Fava) Purée

MAKES ABOUT 2 CUPS

1¼ cups dried broad (fava) beans

cold water, to soak broad beans

3 cloves garlic

3 cups water

¼ cup extra-virgin olive oil

salt

paprika, for garnish

ground cumin, for garnish

Soak the broad beans in cold water for at least 6 hours or overnight. Drain, rinse and skin the broad beans.

Place the broad beans and garlic in a medium-sized saucepan and cover with the water. Bring to a boil, then decrease the heat and gently simmer for 1–1½ hours, until the broad beans are soft.

Purée the broad beans in a food processor or blender. Add the olive oil and stir to combine. Season with salt.

Place in a serving dish and sprinkle with paprika and cumin. Serve warm or cold with bread.

Harissa Paste

MAKES ¾ CUP

1½ ounces dried red chili peppers

boiling water, to cover red chili
  peppers

4 cloves garlic, coarsely chopped

1 teaspoon ground coriander

1 teaspoon ground cumin

¼ teaspoon salt

2 tablespoons olive oil, plus additional
  to cover

Place the dried red chili peppers in a medium-sized bowl and cover with boiling water. Let soak for 1 hour. Drain and coarsely chop.

Place the dried red chili peppers, garlic, coriander, cumin and salt in a food processor or belnder and blend for 10 seconds. Continue blending and gradually add the olive oil in a thin stream until the mixture forms a paste.

Place the harissa in a clean, airtight jar and cover with a thin layer of olive oil. Store in the refrigerator.

❋ Use harissa to marinate meat, poultry or fish, or add it to dressings for a spicier flavor.

❋ Harissa will keep for 2–3 months in the refrigerator.

Chermoula Paste

MAKES ¾ CUP

3 cloves garlic, chopped

½ bunch fresh cilantro, leaves
 chopped

½ bunch fresh flat-leaf parsley, leaves
 chopped

¼ cup olive oil, plus additional to
 cover

¼ cup lemon juice

1½ teaspoons paprika

1 teaspoon ground cumin

1 teaspoon ground coriander

½ teaspoon freshly ground black
 pepper

½ teaspoon salt

Place the garlic, cilantro and parsley in a food processor or blender and blend to a paste. Add the olive oil, lemon juice, spices and salt and blend to combine.

❋ Chermoula is traditionally used to marinate fish and seafood.

❋ Store chermoula in the refrigerator for 2–3 days in an airtight container, covered with a thin layer of olive oil.

Preserved Lemons

MAKES 10–12

boiling water, to prepare preserving
jar

10–12 unwaxed lemons

¾ cup coarse sea salt

½ teaspoon black peppercorns

2 bay leaves

¼ cup lemon juice

boiling water, to cover lemons

Preheat the oven to 240°F. Sterilize a large, 2 quart 4-fluid ounce capacity preserving jar with boiling water and dry out thoroughly in the oven.

Scrub the lemons and rinse well under cold running water.

Cut the lemons in quarters lengthwise, leaving the bottoms intact. Separate the lemon quarters, salt the insides and rejoin the lemon quarters. Pack the lemons, bottoms first to prevent the salt from falling out, into the prepared preserving jar. Scatter with the peppercorns and bay leaves and pour in the lemon juice. Pour in enough boiling water to almost fill the jar. Place a piece of parchment (baking) paper on top of the lemons and weigh this down with something heavy to keep them submerged. Seal the jar and store in a dark place for 1–4 months.

Upon opening, remove and discard the parchment (baking) paper and any white film that has formed on top. Store in the refrigerator.

❈ When using preserved lemons, generally the flesh and membranes are removed and discarded. Rinse the skin and add to tagines and salads. The preserving liquid can be kept and re-used to make your next batch of preserved lemons.

Marinated Olives

½ preserved lemon, quartered, flesh discarded and skin finely sliced lengthwise

2 cups green olives, rinsed

1 cup kalamata olives, rinsed

½ cup olive oil

2 tablespoons lemon juice

2 tablespoons finely chopped fresh flat-leaf parsley

2 tablespoons finely chopped fresh cilantro

1 red chili pepper, deseeded and finely sliced

1 clove garlic, finely sliced

1 teaspoon ground cumin

Place all the ingredients in a medium-sized bowl and stir to combine. Cover and place in the refrigerator for 1–2 days to marinate.

Serve warmed or at room temperature.

Spiced Coffee Mix

MAKES 12 CUPS COFFEE

2 teaspoons ground ginger

1 teaspoon ground nutmeg

1 teaspoon ground cardamom

1 teaspoon ground cinnamon

½ teaspoon ground aniseed

½ teaspoon ground cloves

½ teaspoon freshly ground black
   pepper

Combine all the spices in a small bowl.

To prepare a drink of spiced coffee, combine ¼ teaspoon of spiced coffee mix per cup of coffee with ground coffee. Prepare the coffee as usual, using a French coffee press or drip coffee maker. Refer to manufacturer's instructions if necessary.

❋ You can store this spiced coffee mix in an airtight container in a cool, dark place for up to 2 months.

Spice Mix

Ras el hanout

MAKES 4 TABLESPOONS

3 teaspoons ground nutmeg

2 teaspoons ground cumin

2 teaspoons ground ginger

2 teaspoons freshly ground black
   pepper

1 teaspoon ground coriander

1 teaspoon ground allspice

1 teaspoon ground cardamom

½ teaspoon ground turmeric

½ teaspoon cayenne pepper

¼ teaspoon ground cloves

Combine all the spices in a small bowl.

❉ Ras el hanout is a traditional spice mix containing 10 or more spices. Combinations are
   as varied as the cooks. It is used to flavor tagines, couscous and bastilla.

❉ Store in an airtight container in a cool, dark place for up to 2 months.

Almond Milk

SERVES 4–6

2 cups whole blanched almonds

½ cup superfine sugar

water, to blend almonds and sugar

3 cups milk, chilled

2 teaspoons orange-blossom water

Place the almonds and superfine sugar in a food processor or blender and blend to make a coarse crumb-like consistency. Add 1 cup water and blend for an additional minute. Transfer to a large jar and set aside for 30 minutes to soak.

Add the milk and orange-blossom water to the almond mixture and pass through a fine strainer.

Serve chilled immediately, or as a snack between meals.

Avocado Drink

SERVES 2

1 ripe avocado, pitted

½ cup ice cubes

2 pitted fresh dates, coarsely chopped

1 tablespoon superfine sugar

2 cups milk, chilled

Scoop out the flesh of the avocado and place in a food processor or blender. Add the ice cubes, dates and superfine sugar and blend for 30 seconds. Add half of the milk and blend for an additional 30 seconds, until smooth. Add the remaining milk and blend to combine.

Serve chilled immediately, or as a snack between meals.

Peach Milkshake

Sharbat

SERVES 4

2 large ripe peaches

water, to blanch peaches

2 cups chilled milk

½ cup iced water

2 tablespoons superfine sugar

½ teaspoon rosewater

ground cinnamon, for sprinkling

Score a cross at the bottom of each of the peaches. Bring a pot of water to a boil and blanch the peaches quickly, then plunge into iced water. Peel and discard the skin from the peaches, and roughly chop the flesh.

Put the peaches and the remaining ingredients in a blender or food processor, and blend until combined well.

Pour into chilled glasses and sprinkle with a little cinnamon to serve.

Moroccan Mint Tea

SERVES 2–3

1 tablespoon Chinese gunpowder
  green tea

water, to cover tea

6 sprigs fresh spearmint

3–4 sugar cubes (or to taste)

2 cups boiling water

Place the green tea in a medium-sized teapot (capacity about 17-fluid ounces) suitable for the stovetop. Just cover the tea with water. Set over low–medium heat and bring to a boil. Discard the water but retain the tea in the teapot. Refill the teapot with fresh water to three-quarters full, return to the heat and bring to a boil. Remove from the heat, add the fresh spearmint and sugar cubes and set aside to steep for 3 minutes.

Pour some of the tea into two small glasses, then return it to the teapot (this helps to combine the flavors). Taste the tea for sweetness and add more sugar cubes if desired. Serve in small tea glasses, poured from a height to expose to air.

❊ The Moroccan tea ceremony is preformed in front of guests. The tea is boiled, poured, discarded, and re-poured always from a height.

❊ Other herbs, such as thyme, can be used to make Moroccan tea, but spearmint is the most widely used. Either fresh or dried spearmint can be used depending on availability and individual taste.

Special Ingredients

AMALOU This almond and honey spread is easy to make and keeps for up to three weeks.

CHEBBAKIA Moroccan sesame cookie, folded into a flower shape, fried and covered with honey.

CHERMOULA A dry spice mix traditionally used to marinate fish and seafood. It can be purchased from specialty markets.

CHINESE GUNPOWDER TEA A green tea of granular appearance. The tightly rolled leaves have a refreshing taste, especially when added to preparations for Moroccan mint tea.

HARISSA A chili pepper-based hot sauce used to flavor many Moroccan dishes. It can be easily made or purchased from most supermarkets.

KEFTA Ground meat, particularly beef or lamb, or in combination.

MARSHMALLOW LEAVES Readily available at Moroccan markets when in season, this plant can be difficult to find outside of Morocco. Spinach is an appropriate substitute.

ORANGE-BLOSSOM WATER (orange-flower water) A solution of orange-blossom oil in water. Used mainly as a flavoring in desserts.

PRESERVED LEMONS When using preserved lemons, generally the pulp and membrane are removed and discarded. Rinse the skin and add to tagines and salads.

RAS EL HANOUT A Middle Eastern spice mix containing 10 or more spices. Combinations are as varied as the cooks. The recipes in this book use the blend common to Moroccan cooking on page 242. Ready-made versions can be purchased from most supermarkets.

ROSEWATER A scented water made with rose petals, used to add a distinctive aroma and flavor to food, especially sweets.

SAFFRON A small amount of saffron threads is enough to add brilliant yellow color, delicate fragrance and distinctive flavor.

WARKA PASTRY A paper-thin Moroccan pastry sold in large rounds resembling crêpes. It is used in Moroccan cooking to make dishes such as bastilla and briouats. For frying, spring-roll wrappers make a good substitute. For baking, filo pastry is more suitable – spring-roll wrappers tend to become rubbery when baked.

Index

PENGUIN BOOKS

Published by the Penguin Group
Penguin Group (USA) Inc., 375 Hudson Street, New York, New York 10014, USA
Penguin Group (Canada), 90 Eglinton Avenue East, Suite 700, Toronto, Ontario M4P 2Y3, Canada
(a division of Pearson Penguin Canada Inc.)
Penguin Books Ltd, 80 Strand, London WC2R 0RL, England
Penguin Ireland, 25 St Stephen's Green, Dublin 2, Ireland (a division of Penguin Books Ltd)
Penguin Group (Australia), 707 Collins Street, Melbourne, Victoria 3008, Australia
(a division of Pearson Australia Group Pty Ltd)
Penguin Books India Pvt Ltd, 11 Community Centre, Panchsheel Park, New Delhi–110 017, India
Penguin Group (NZ), 67 Apollo Drive, Rosedale, Auckland 0632, New Zealand (a division of Pearson New Zealand Ltd)
Penguin Books (South Africa), Rosebank Office Park, 181 Jan Smuts Avenue, Parktown North 2193, South Africa
Penguin China, B7 Jiaming Center, 27 East Third Ring Road North, Chaoyang District, Beijing 100020, China

Penguin Books Ltd, Registered Offices: 80 Strand, London WC2R 0RL, England

Previously published in Australia as *Moroccan Bible* under ISBN 978-0-14-320293-6

This edition published in 2012 by Penguin Group (USA) Inc.
Special Markets ISBN 978-0-14-242501-5

10 9 8 7 6 5 4 3 2

Text and photographs copyright © Penguin Group (Australia), 2010

Written by Rachael Lane

Designed by Claire Tice and Marley Flory © Penguin Group (Australia)
Photography by Julie Renouf
Food styling by Lee Blaylock
Scans and separations by Splitting Image, P/L, Clayton, Victoria
Printed in the United States of America